Searching for Happiness

Also by Martin Thielen
from Westminster John Knox Press

*The Answer to Bad Religion Is Not No Religion: A Guide
to Good Religion for Seekers, Skeptics, and Believers*

*The Answer to Bad Religion Is Not No Religion: A Guide
to Good Religion for Seekers, Skeptics, and Believers —
Leader's Guide* (with Jessica Miller Kelley)

*The Answer to Bad Religion Is Not No Religion: A Guide
to Good Religion for Seekers, Skeptics, and Believers —
Outreach Kit* (with Jessica Miller Kelley)

*What's the Least I Can Believe and Still Be a Christian: A Guide
to What Matters Most, New Edition with Study Guide*

Searching for Happiness

*How Generosity, Faith,
and Other Spiritual Habits
Can Lead to a Full Life*

MARTIN THIELEN

WJK WESTMINSTER
JOHN KNOX PRESS
LOUISVILLE · KENTUCKY

© 2016 Martin Thielen

First edition
Published by Westminster John Knox Press
Louisville, Kentucky

16 17 18 19 20 21 22 23 24 25—10 9 8 7 6 5 4 3 2 1

Unless otherwise indicated, Scripture quotations are from the New Revised Standard Version of the Bible, copyright © 1989 by the Division of Christian Education of the National Council of the Churches of Christ in the U.S.A., and are used by permission.

Scripture quotations marked NIV are from the Holy Bible, New International Version. Copyright © 1973, 1978, 1984, 2011 by Biblica, Inc. ® Used by permission. All rights reserved worldwide.

Scripture quotations marked NLT are taken from the Holy Bible, New Living Translation, copyright 1996, 2004. Used by permission of Tyndale House Publishers, Inc., Wheaton, Illinois 60189. All rights reserved.

Scripture verses marked TLB are taken from The Living Bible © 1971. Used by permission of Tyndale House Publishers, Inc., Wheaton, IL 60189. All rights reserved.

Book design by Drew Stevens
Cover design by Marc Whitaker / MTWdesign.net

Library of Congress Cataloging-in-Publication Data

Thielen, Martin, 1956-
    Searching for happiness : how generosity, faith, and other spiritual habits can lead to a full life / Martin Thielen.
       pages cm
    Includes bibliographical references.
    ISBN 978-0-664-23712-7 (alk. paper)
    1. Contentment—Religious aspects—Christianity. 2. Happiness—Religious aspects—Christianity. 3. Christian life. I. Title.
    BV4647.C7T45 2016
    248.4—dc23
                                                                              2015028288

Most Westminster John Knox Press books are available at special quantity discounts when purchased in bulk by corporations, organizations, and special-interest groups. For more information, please e-mail SpecialSales@wjkbooks.com.

*To my wife, Paula, our children, Jonathan and Laura,
and their spouses, Erin and Philip, and our granddaughter, Anna,
all of whom bring great joy and contentment to my life.*

CONTENTS

PREFACE

Years ago a successful, affluent, attractive woman with a picture-perfect family came to visit me. Her name was Sarah. A few minutes into the visit, Sarah began to cry her heart out. She told me that she had serious marital problems, major conflicts with her grown daughter, and overwhelming stress at work. During the conversation I asked her, "What do you most want out of life?"

With tears rolling down her face, Sarah said, "I just want to be happy." After she regained her composure, we sat in silence for a moment. I could sense a debate going on in her mind. Finally, she decided to risk complete vulnerability. Sarah said: "I make a lot of money. I'm successful in my profession. And people tell me that I'm attractive. Yet I'm terribly unhappy. So I want to know—if money, success, and beauty don't make you happy, what does?"

My conversation with Sarah occurred over twenty years ago. Since then I've discovered important insights into what makes people content. I'm now ready to answer Sarah's question with a strong degree of confidence. For example, I've learned that although it sounds counterintuitive, Sarah is correct. Money, success, beauty, and other external circumstances don't make people happy. Although that statement is a hard sell in America, in chapter 1, we'll see why it's true. In chapters 2–10, we'll explore nine things that actually do make people happy. However, before we begin, it's important to clarify that happiness is *not* the ultimate goal of Christianity. It does not rate up there with the Ten Commandments, the prophet's call for justice, the Great Commandment, or advancement of the kingdom of God. But the quest for authentic contentment—which every heart longs for and every person seeks—leads us to significant Christian themes, including relationships, generosity, forgiveness, gratitude, and faith, as we'll see in the following pages.

The conclusions in this book about achieving life satisfaction come from three primary sources: (1) theological and biblical teachings, especially from the Old Testament book of Ecclesiastes and the New Testament book of Philippians, (2) scientific research from the emerging discipline of "positive psychology," and (3) my own experience, both professionally and personally. This book contains more personal disclosure than anything I've ever written before. However, I've learned a lot about contentment over the past few decades, and I want to share some of those insights. In short, this book will explore what Scripture, science, and my own experience teach about contentment.

Each chapter will include questions for study and reflection along with a challenge activity. At the back of the book is a brief study guide to help you use this in a group setting.

Before proceeding further, a brief clarification needs to be made. Throughout the following chapters I use the terms "happiness," "contentment," and "life satisfaction." For the purposes of this book, these words are interchangeable. Rather than offering nuances of meaning, their only purpose is to offer variety in language. However, it's important to note that in every case, these terms refer to *internal* well-being rather than *external* well-being, as chapter 1 fully explains.

So turn the page and let's explore Sarah's provocative question, "If money, success, and beauty don't make people happy, what does?"

CHAPTER 1

CONTENTED PEOPLE
KNOW THAT EXTERNAL
CIRCUMSTANCES DON'T
DETERMINE HAPPINESS

I kept my heart from no pleasure. . . . I . . . had great possessions. . . .
I made great works. . . . Then I considered all that my hands had done
and the toil I had spent in doing it, and again, all was vanity and a
chasing after wind.

—Ecclesiastes 2:10, 7, 4, 11

A familiar voice on the other end of the phone said, "Hi, Martin. It's Larry. I'm in Nashville for a few days at a conference, and I wondered if we could have lunch together." Larry, a clergy friend, serves as senior pastor at a large church in the South. At the time of his call, I worked at the denominational headquarters of my old church. The next day we met at a Mexican restaurant in West Nashville. We talked a long time about our work, our families, and the politics raging in our denomination.

1

The time quickly passed, and I assumed our visit was nearly over. But then, in a rare moment of transparency and honesty, Larry shared something that caught me completely off guard. He said, "For the past several years, I've been struggling with a strong spirit of discontentment." That revelation surprised me. From my limited perspective, Larry lived a charmed life. A handsome, intelligent, and outgoing man, he served a large and respected church in his home state. His wife, an attractive woman who sings like an angel, is smart, kind, and exceptionally funny. They have two beautiful and gifted children. On top of all that, Larry's wife came from a wealthy family, so money never posed a problem. And yet, in spite of all those blessings, Larry told me he rarely felt satisfied and had no inner peace. Concerned he might have clinical depression, he went to see a psychiatrist. However, the doctor told him he did not suffer from clinical depression and did not need antidepressant medication. Still Larry struggled daily with restlessness and discontentment.

An Inside Job

Larry told me that at first he assumed the problem was his church. He thought, *If only I could get a bigger and better church, then I would be content.* But Larry got a bigger and better church, and it didn't help. As soon as the initial excitement wore off, Larry felt just as discontented as before. Since the problem wasn't his church, Larry figured the problem must be his career. He thought he must be in the wrong profession. So he went to a top-flight career counselor, took a battery of aptitude tests, and engaged in numerous vocational interviews. But in the end he realized the problem wasn't his career. In fact, he discovered he was extremely well suited for pastoral work. After extensive evaluation,

Larry's career counselor told him, "I can't think of a better vocation for you than serving as a minister."

Larry finally said to me: "It's taken several years and numerous counseling sessions, but I've learned something extremely important. I've finally figured out that the problem is not my church or my vocation—but *me*. I've learned that my restlessness and discontentment are not an external problem but an internal problem. I've learned that happiness is an inside job."

Although it took significant effort, my friend Larry learned that external circumstances, including our jobs, have little impact on overall life satisfaction. In fact, external circumstances, including our job, money, house, and personal appearance, account for only a small fraction of a person's happiness. I know that's hard to believe, especially in America, but it's absolutely true. Science, experience, and Scripture all clearly teach that happiness is indeed, in Larry's words, "an inside job." However, given the counterintuitive nature of this claim, I don't expect you to accept it at face value. So let's explore the evidence.

The Scientific Evidence

Like many of you, I vividly remember my freshman year of college. One of my first classes was Psychology 101. In that class we studied clinical depression, bipolar disorder, schizophrenia, dysfunctional families, eating disorders, addictions, and other cheery topics! Over the past fifty years, the science of psychology primarily focused on pathologies—things that make people sick and miserable. But in recent years a growing number of psychologists have been studying what is called "positive psychology." Positive psychology focuses not on pathologies but on what makes people healthy and happy. For almost two decades, leading psychologists at highly respected institutions like Harvard, Stanford, and the University of California have carefully studied happiness. For a comprehensive overview of this fascinating research, I recommend that you read *The How of Happiness: A New Approach to Getting the Life You Want* by Dr. Sonja Lyubomirsky, professor of psychology at the University of California, Riverside, whom I will cite extensively throughout this book. She's written a follow-up book called *The Myths of Happiness: What Should Make You Happy but Doesn't, What Shouldn't Make You Happy, but Does.*[1]

The most interesting conclusion of positive psychology research is how little external circumstances impact life satisfaction. Most people believe life circumstances are the primary key to happiness. For example, if we took a survey of average Americans and asked, "What would make you happier?" they would likely list things like:

- Find a better job.
- Make more money.
- Own a nicer house.
- Have a more loving partner.
- Lose a lot of weight.
- Have a child.
- Be more physically attractive.
- Be a prominent member of the community.
- Inherit a large estate.

Most people believe that if we can get our circumstances just right, happiness will follow. However, positive psychologists have discovered this is a myth. Circumstances play a small role in happiness. In fact, life circumstances — including income, health, physical appearance, and marital status — account for only about 10 percent of a person's overall life satisfaction.

Take money, for example. Many people think, *If I can just get enough money, I'll be happy.* But that's not true. Extensive research has proven that after our basic needs are met, additional money has minimal impact on our happiness. In his book *Flourish*, Martin Seligman, a psychologist and an expert in happiness studies, cites amazing research. Pennsylvania Amish, Inuit people in northern Greenland, and African Masai—people who have minimal income and few material assets—have virtually the same levels of life satisfaction as *Forbes* magazine's richest Americans.[2] In spite of beliefs to the contrary, after our core necessities are met, money does not make people happy.

Neither does physical beauty. Although many of us believe beautiful people are happier than plain people, research has proven otherwise. Numerous studies have shown that attractive people are no happier than average-looking people. For example, one psychologist tells about a woman who had major cosmetic surgery on her face, including eye lifts, a face lift, a nose job, liposuction under her chin, and laser resurfacing of her skin. The surgery made her look younger and more attractive. But a year later she said: "I do have to say it's nice to have less wrinkles. But it didn't make me happier. The makeover is nothing compared to *real* happiness."[3] Beauty, like money, does not make people happy. Neither does fame, children, a status job, youthfulness, or intelligence. Even good health doesn't make people more appreciably happy. In the end, external circumstances have minimal impact on happiness. It accounts for only about 10 percent of overall life satisfaction.

Although I'd like to go into far more depth on this subject, we have much more to cover. However, in order to give you a taste of the fascinating research on this important topic, I've listed the following quotes from three leading experts on the subject of happiness:

Lyubomirsky, in *The How of Happiness*, says:

- "The things most of us think create happiness—wealth, fame, beauty—don't really matter all that much."[4]
- "Changes in our circumstances, no matter how positive and stunning, actually have little bearing on our well-being."[5]
- "Not only does materialism not bring happiness, but it's been shown to be a strong predictor of unhappiness."[6]
- "Beautiful people are not happier than their plain-looking relatives, colleagues, and friends."[7]
- "Although you may find it very hard to believe, whether you drive to work in a Lexus hybrid or a battered truck, whether you're young or old, or have had wrinkle-removing plastic surgery, whether you live in the frigid Midwest or on the balmy West Coast, your chances of being happy and becoming happier are pretty much the same."[8]
- "Trying to be happy by changing our life situations ultimately will not work."[9]

Richard Layard, economist, happiness expert, and author of *Happiness: Lessons from a New Science*, states:

- "Most people want more income and strive for it. Yet as Western societies have got richer, their people have become no happier."[10]
- "For most types of people in the West, happiness has not increased since 1950. In the United States people are no happier, although living standards have more than doubled."[11]
- "When whole societies have become richer, they have not become happier."[12]
- "Depression has actually increased as incomes have risen."[13]

- "We have in the First World a deep paradox—a society that seeks and delivers ever greater income, but is little if any happier than before."[14]
- "We can begin with five features that on average have a negligible effect on happiness . . . age . . . gender . . . looks . . . IQ . . . education."[15]

Martin Seligman, who also wrote *Authentic Happiness*, claims:

- "The less fortunate are, by and large, just as happy as the more fortunate. Good things and high accomplishments, studies have shown, have astonishingly little power to raise happiness more than transiently."[16]
- "Rich people are, on average, only slightly happier than poor people."[17]
- "Physical attractiveness . . . does not have much effect at all on happiness."[18]
- "Objective physical health, perhaps the most valuable of all resources, is barely correlated with happiness."[19]
- "Once a person is just barely comfortable, added money adds little or no happiness. Even the fabulously rich—the *Forbes* 100, with an average net worth of over 125 million dollars—are only slightly happier than the average American."[20]
- "Surprisingly, none of them (education, intelligence, climate, gender and race) much matters for happiness."[21]

The research is clear. In the end, external circumstances have little impact on life satisfaction. Of course, they can make a short-term impact on our happiness. If we win the lottery, we will be extremely happy but only for a short while. For example, a classic study of Illinois State Lottery winners (people who won between fifty thousand and one million dollars in 1970s dollars) revealed an amazing fact. Less than a year after winning the lottery, winners were no happier than regular folks who did not have the good fortune of receiving a windfall of money.[22] The same dynamic is true with getting a new house or car, getting engaged or married, having a child, or getting a promotion. These things will briefly raise our happiness, but it wears off rapidly. Bottom line: psychological research has proven that circumstances do not significantly increase long-term contentment.

The Experiential Evidence

As we've seen, psychological research reveals that external circumstances do not impact happiness in any significant way. Experience also supports that conclusion. Many rich, beautiful, and famous people live miserable lives of broken relationships, substance abuse, and crippling, sometimes suicidal, depression. For example, while I was writing this book, the talented and wildly successful comedian and actor Robin Williams tragically took his own life. On the other hand, a lot of simple, economically modest, and average-looking people live lives full of joy and happiness. No significant correlation exists between external circumstances and life satisfaction.

I've worked in pastoral ministry for over three decades. I've served small churches with hundreds of members, large churches with over a thousand members, and a megachurch with ten thousand members (adults and children). My profession constantly puts me in close contact with large numbers of people. After decades of pastoral experience, one thing has become overwhelmingly clear to me: external circumstances like money, status, success, popularity, beautiful homes, personal appearance, education levels, and IQ have little impact on life satisfaction. Some

of the most miserable people I've known are rich, successful, attractive, well educated, and prominent. On the other
hand, some of the happiest people I've known have few
financial assets, minimal social status, average physical
appearance, and even poor health. After decades of being
in the people business, I've seen firsthand the extremely
small correlation between external circumstances and
contentment.

Not only has this been true in my professional life, but
it's also been true in my personal life. In one of my previous
books, *What's the Least I Can Believe and Still Be a Christian?*, I
confessed that in my early adult years I chased after money
in the business world and then chased after success in the
church world. Although I attained some degree of wealth
and success, it never satisfied my desire for contentment.
Finally, through a series of life-changing events and a powerful epiphany, I finally realized, like my friend Larry, that
contentment is not dependent on external circumstances
but is "an inside job." For over twenty years I've been
highly content, regardless of the circumstances.

Instructively, the least contented professional experience of my life—although I still maintained a good bit of
personal contentment—occurred during a two-year stint
as senior pastor of a megachurch. It was the largest church
of my denomination in my state and one of the largest in
the nation. It represented the pinnacle of my career—an
extremely high-status and high-salary job. The church
enjoyed exceptional facilities, a massive staff, a huge membership, and impressive ministries and programs. The job
even came with a company car. I had "arrived" in my profession. Ironically, I did not like the job. The shift from a
pastoral role to a CEO role proved a difficult fit. The daily
complexities of leading a huge organization exhausted me.
The sky-high expectations to be an ideal preacher, leader,
and pastor felt impossible to fulfill. Conflict, inevitable in all

congregations, grows exponentially with size and took away much of the joy of ministry. Finally, the relentless criticism that comes from being in such a public and high-profile job took a toll on me. It didn't take long in that setting for me to realize that I enjoyed smaller, less status, and less paying pastorates far more than the megachurch. I vividly learned through that experience that *external circumstances like status and salary have virtually no bearing on happiness*. I know from both professional and personal experience — external circumstances do not make people happy.

The Scriptural Evidence

Both science and experience affirm that external circumstances do not make much of a dent in personal happiness. Scripture teaches the same truth. Although many examples could be given, perhaps the best come from the Old Testament book of Ecclesiastes.

The writer of Ecclesiastes reminds me of an unusual cartoon I once saw. The cartoon depicts a cow wearing fine jewelry and drinking a cocktail with her husband, a bull named Wendell. She tells him, "Wendell, I'm not content." That's the story of Ecclesiastes. In spite of positive external circumstances — like affluence, status, and power — for most of his life, the writer of Ecclesiastes (who is not identified in the book) was not happy. Instead, he felt exceptionally unhappy. Why? Because he sought contentment through external circumstances, including education, entertainment, possessions, and career success. Thankfully, the writer of Ecclesiastes — called "the Teacher" — eventually realized that happiness was "an inside job," and he turned to more fruitful contentment strategies, which we will explore later in this book. But before traveling down these more productive paths, he unsuccessfully searched for happiness in all the wrong places.

Ecclesiastes begins by reviewing four popular but ultimately dead-end paths people often travel in their quest for a contented life. The writer of Ecclesiastes spent most of his adult life walking down these four paths. However, these external efforts to find happiness did not satisfy him, so he warns his readers not to follow his example. If we'll heed Ecclesiastes' warning to steer clear of these paths as a means for finding happiness, we can avoid a lot of unnecessary pain and wasted time. Let's review all four paths.

1. The Path of Philosophy. In chapter 1, the writer of Ecclesiastes said, "I said to myself, 'I have acquired great wisdom, surpassing all who were over Jerusalem before me; and my mind has had great experience of wisdom and knowledge'" (v. 16). In his quest for happiness, Ecclesiastes turned to education, wisdom, and knowledge.

Philosophy is still a popular path to follow today. Many people believe they can find ultimate meaning in life through education and knowledge. But as we've already seen, the path of philosophy has little impact on life satisfaction. As Seligman notes in his book *Authentic Happiness*, intelligence and education make almost no positive impact on happiness levels. His research shows that education "is not a means to higher happiness . . . nor does intelligence influence happiness in either direction."[23] The Teacher of Ecclesiastes came to the same conclusion. As he reflected on his efforts to gain knowledge and wisdom, he said, "For in much wisdom is much vexation, and those who increase knowledge increase sorrow" (1:18). Since he could not find happiness in his mind, the Teacher tried to find it in his body, as we'll see in the second path he followed on his quest for contentment.

2. The Path of Pleasure. In chapter 2 the writer of Ecclesiastes said, "Come now, I will make a test of pleasure; enjoy yourself.' . . . I searched with my mind how to cheer my body with wine. . . . I got singers . . . and delights of the flesh, and many concubines. . . . Whatever my eyes desired I did not keep from them; I kept my heart from no pleasure" (2:1, 3, 8, 10).

In his quest for contentment, the writer of Ecclesiastes looked to numerous forms of pleasure. For example, he indulged in wine, music, and women. Today people still turn to pleasure to find contentment. And they still look to wine, music, and women—and a host of other pleasures, both healthy and destructive. However, in the end this path does not deliver on its promise to bring happiness. As Seligman said, "The 'pleasant life' might be had by drinking champagne and driving a Porsche, but not the good life."[24]

When my son, Jonathan, was a boy, I took him to the county fair. He talked me into riding the Tilt-A-Whirl. For a while it was fun. But the ride went on and on. People frantically screamed at the ride man to stop the ride. But he just sat there, staring at us with a sadistic smile. He kept spinning us around for what seemed like hours. Jonathan and I felt desperately sick. Finally he stopped the ride. If I hadn't been so sick and if I hadn't been the pastor of First Church, I would have punched this guy out! Pleasure works the same way. It's enjoyable for a while and can even be good and healthy. We all need diversions and fun. But if all we have is another trip to the fair or another vacation to plan or another football game or concert to attend—if pleasure is all we have—it's like a carnival ride that never ends, leaving us dissatisfied and ill. As the writer of Ecclesiastes said sarcastically, "I said of . . . pleasure, 'What use is it?'" (2:2). Pleasure, by itself, is not enough. Since pleasure did not satisfy his deep longing for contentment, the Teacher of Ecclesiastes tried a third path.

3. *The Path of Possessions*. The Teacher of Ecclesiastes said, "I also had great possessions of herds and flocks, more than any who had been before me in Jerusalem. I

also gathered for myself silver and gold and the treasure of kings" (2:7–8).

In America accumulating possessions is a highly popular path for finding contentment. Somehow we believe acquiring more things will add meaning to our lives. We think if we can just get a bigger house, a newer car, a home theater system, or a bigger stock portfolio, then we'll be happy. But as we've already seen, the path of possessions doesn't work. For example, social scientists have long studied contentment levels among nations. Fifty years ago Americans were the most contented people on earth. Since then we have raised the standard of living in this country in amazing ways. We are the most affluent people in the world. We live in big houses, drive high-quality cars, have TVs and computers in every room, own closets full of clothes, and own every electronic gadget imaginable. But in recent years major studies have revealed that America is no longer the most contented nation on earth. In spite of all the stuff we've purchased, America has fallen from the most contented nation in the world to a far less contented country. In spite of all our consumption, and the environmental damage it took to produce it, we are less satisfied with life, not more. Having lots of possessions does not lead to contentment. No matter how much stuff we get, contentment remains elusive.

I'm not naive about money. We are economic creatures and need at least some possessions. Nobody can live a quality life without having basic needs met. But once our core necessities are met, more stuff will not satisfy the deep longing in our souls for meaning and satisfaction. The idea that more stuff buys happiness is an American myth and lie that the American church needs to challenge. In short, materialism just doesn't work. The writer of Ecclesiastes learned that. He said of all his possessions, "Everything was meaningless, a chasing after the wind" (2:11 NIV).

In chapter 5 he adds, "Whoever loves money never has enough; whoever loves wealth is never satisfied with their income" (5:10 NIV). So far the writer of Ecclesiastes has tried three paths in his quest for a meaningful life. None satisfied his longing for purpose, meaning, happiness, and contentment. So he tried a fourth path.

4. The Path of Production. The Teacher of Ecclesiastes said, "I made great works. . . . I became great and surpassed all who were before me in Jerusalem" (2:4, 9). Since philosophy, pleasure, and possessions did not bring him contentment, the Teacher looked to his career, his successes, and his accomplishments. He said, "I made great works."

Production is probably the most popular path Americans follow to find contentment. They constantly try to find meaning and happiness through their careers. But once again this path does not work. As Seligman notes, "High accomplishments . . . have astonishingly little power to raise happiness more than transiently."[25] The writer of Ecclesiastes learned the hard reality that career success, in spite of its many benefits, does not bring happiness. He put incredible energy into the path of production. He made it to the top. He produced. He became highly successful. But all that success did not give him the meaning and contentment he sought. In one of the saddest verses in the Bible, he said, "When I surveyed all that my hands had done and what I had toiled to achieve, everything was meaningless, a chasing after the wind; nothing was gained under the sun" (2:11 NIV). In the end the Teacher finally realized that career production and success are not the secret of a contented life.

Late in his life the writer of Ecclesiastes realized that the four paths he had spent most of his life traveling — the paths of philosophy, pleasure, possessions, and production — were ultimately bankrupt in terms of producing happiness. They could not satisfy; they could not offer contentment. Each path promised far more than it could deliver.

Please don't misunderstand what I'm saying. I'm not suggesting that these four things are unimportant, because they are. Everyone needs some education. Everyone needs some pleasure in life. Everyone needs at least some possessions. And everyone needs to be productive in some way. We all need to work, either on the job, at home, or in a volunteer capacity. Work is a crucial part of life. So while these four paths are all important, they are not the secrets of happiness. Why? Because contentment does not come from external circumstances. Instead, contentment is "an inside job."

Lost in the Forest

The Teacher's story reminds me of a rabbinical story about a man who went for a walk in the forest. After walking for a while, he became hopelessly lost. He wandered around for hours, going down one path and then the other, but none of them led out of the forest. Then abruptly he came across another hiker walking through the forest. He cried out: "Thank God for another human being! Can you show me the path that leads back to town?"

The other man replied: "No, I'm lost, too. But we can help each other in this way. We can tell each other which paths we walked down that led nowhere, and through the process of elimination, we can figure out the path that leads home."

That's exactly what the writer of Ecclesiastes does in his book. He tells us that the path of philosophy, pleasure, possessions, and production (external circumstances) are not the secrets of a contented life. Thankfully, Ecclesiastes also shares some right paths on the journey toward contentment, and we'll review those later in the book. But for now it's crucial to understand that external circumstances do not determine life satisfaction and happiness.

The 90 Percent

A few final notes are in order before moving on. We've already said that circumstances amount to only 10 percent of a person's happiness. That raises the question: What about the other 90 percent? Although some people are discouraged to learn it, genetics plays a major role in a person's happiness. In fact, research has shown that 50 percent of a person's overall happiness is genetic. Every person has a genetic "set point" of happiness that is inborn and does not change, regardless of circumstances or behaviors. While 50 percent is significant, thankfully it's not 100 percent. This means you and I still have a good bit of control in determining our overall life satisfaction.

The remaining 40 percent of a person's happiness levels is the direct result of our attitudes and behaviors, which, unlike genetics, we can control. Although 40 percent is not a massive number, it does mean we can have a major impact on our happiness. In short, the attitudes we foster and the behaviors we follow will make a significant impact on our contentment.

The rest of this book will focus on the 40 percent of happiness we can influence. Since we cannot control our genetics, there's no sense worrying about that. And since circumstances have such little impact on happiness and many of our circumstances are beyond our control, there's no use spending time on that either. But you and I have full control over the 40 percent. For example, let's say we have a low genetic set point for happiness, along with difficult life circumstances. If so, perhaps we have only a 30 percent happiness grade. Back when I went to school, that was an F minus on the grading scale. But, we can add 40 percent to that low score, bringing us up to 70 percent, which is at least a C minus! The point is that we can have a strong impact on our overall contentment level by intentionally practicing attitudes and behaviors that lead to happiness.

This 40 percent factor is what I find most interesting. After years of extensive research, psychologists have discovered at least nine practices—all of which are under our control—that lead to happiness. What I find especially compelling is that all nine of those happiness traits are taught in the Bible, as we'll see in chapters ahead. They are also confirmed by experience. So when it comes to overall life contentment, science, experience, and Scripture are in complete agreement. The following nine attitudes and behaviors make people content:

1. Contented people use trials as growth opportunities.
2. Contented people cultivate optimism.
3. Contented people focus on the present.
4. Contented people practice forgiveness.
5. Contented people practice generosity.
6. Contented people nurture relationships.
7. Contented people express gratitude.
8. Contented people care for their bodies.
9. Contented people care for their souls.

To these nine traits we will now turn our attention.

CHAPTER 2

CONTENTED PEOPLE USE TRIALS AS GROWTH OPPORTUNITIES

Consider it pure joy, my brothers and sisters, whenever you face trials of many kinds, because you know that the testing of your faith produces perseverance. Let perseverance finish its work so that you may be mature and complete, not lacking anything.

—James 1:2–4 NIV

During the Civil War battle of Shiloh, a young Union soldier suffered a serious bullet wound to his arm. When his captain saw what happened, he said, "Private, give me your gun, then run north to the rear of the battle." The private handed the captain his gun and ran north. However, when he arrived, fighting raged all around him. So he ran west, but the battle raged there as well. Still seeking the rear of the battle, the wounded private ran east. But once again he found himself in a fiercely pitched battle zone. Finally the private ran back to his captain. He said, "Captain, give me back my gun. There ain't no rear to this battle!"

The famous Swiss psychiatrist Carl Jung once said: "Life is a battleground. It always will be, and if it were not so, existence would come to an end." Like that young, wounded Union soldier, we cannot run away from the battle. Struggles and trials are an inescapable part of life. Scripture teaches us that nobody is exempt from troubles, not even faithful believers. In the book of Job we read, "Mortals, born of woman, are of few days and full of trouble" (Job 14:1 NIV). Jesus told his disciples in the Gospel of John, "In this world you will have trouble" (John 16:33 NIV). Happy people, therefore, do not avoid pain, sorrow, trials, and trouble—that's impossible. Instead, happy people learn to use trials as opportunities for growth.

Survive or Thrive?

How people respond to life's trials determines, in large measure, how happy they will be. For example, positive psychologist Sonja Lyubomirsky cites important research on dealing with adversity. According to Lyubomirsky, psychological research has discovered that when people face a major crisis in life, they do one of three things. They either (1) survive, (2) recover, or (3) thrive. People who *survive* find a way to go on after the crisis, but their life is significantly diminished. People who *recover* suffer for a while, but eventually they are able to return to the life satisfaction and happiness level they had before the crisis. People who *thrive* suffer just as much as those who survive or recover, but they go beyond mere survival or recovery. Instead, they use their crisis to grow, learn, mature, and become a better person. Research has proven that these people, people who use trials as growth opportunities, are far happier than those who just survive or recover.[1]

A Tale of Two Couples

I once heard about two midlife couples who share a tragic story. Fifteen years ago one of the couples had a teenage son and the other had a teenage daughter. Their two children were high school sweethearts. On the night of their senior prom, this teenage couple had a terrible automobile accident. One died instantly; the other died the next day. Both sets of parents suffered through a terrible year of grief. However, a year later they had to decide what to do next. The two couples followed different paths. The couple whose son died chose to live their life in the past. They held tightly to their grief and despair. Today, fifteen years later, their son's room is just like it was on the night he died. It serves as a sort of eternal shrine to their endless pain. Although they go through the motions of living, they are dead inside; no joy or laughter exists in their home.

The couple whose daughter died chose a different path. Although they loved their daughter more than life itself and their grief over her death was enormous, they decided to live again. They serve as active leaders of their church youth group, they regularly host foreign exchange students, and their lives are full of joy and contentment. It's not that they have forgotten their grief. They still cry occasional tears and sometimes struggle with deep feelings of loss. But rather than spend their life living in past grief, they made the decision to move forward with gratitude, hope, and faith.

Using Lyubomirsky's terminology above, the first couple chose to *survive*. The second couple, however, chose to *recover* and eventually to *thrive*. As you might expect, the first couple experience virtually no joy or happiness in their lives. The second couple, in spite of their great loss, experience great happiness in their lives.

A Crucial Choice

I'm not suggesting that thriving after a crisis is simple, easy, or quickly accomplished. The loss of a loved one, the collapse of a marriage, the death of a dream, or the onset of a serious illness is overwhelmingly painful. In such circumstances we cannot simply "pick ourselves up by our bootstraps" and happily move forward. Instead, we must give ourselves time to grieve and then grieve some more. We also need to seek support from others, perhaps even a professional counselor. But eventually a crucial decision must be made. Will we only survive the trial? Will we simply recover? Or will we choose to thrive? Scientific research tells us that people who choose to thrive are far happier than those who merely survive or recover.

Scripture concurs with psychology. The Bible consistently challenges us to emerge from trials stronger and more mature than we were before the struggle. Scripture further teaches that when we do we will be happier and more content, as we see in the following two passages:

- "Consider it pure *joy*, my brothers and sisters, whenever you face trials of many kinds, because you know that the testing of your faith produces perseverance. Let perseverance finish its work so that you may be mature and complete, not lacking anything." (Jas. 1:2–4 NIV, emphasis added)
- "We also *glory* in our sufferings, because we know that suffering produces perseverance; perseverance, character; and character, hope. And hope does not put us to shame." (Rom. 5:3–5 NIV, emphasis added)

The Bible is clear. Using trials as growth opportunities brings joy into our lives. Both Scripture and science agree on this matter. If we want to be happy, we must learn to turn trials into opportunities of growth.

Contentment in Adversity

The Bible tells many stories about people growing through adversity. A good example is the apostle Paul. We learn in 2 Corinthians 12 that Paul suffered from a physical aliment he called "a thorn in the flesh." We don't know what Paul's ailment was. Some scholars believe he had epilepsy. Whatever his thorn was, Paul hated it and asked God to remove it from his life. He said, "Three times I pleaded with the Lord to take it away from me" (v. 8 NIV). But God did not remove Paul's thorn.

Some problems we must learn to live with regardless of our faith. When God did not remove his physical ailment, Paul began to see it in a different light. He came to realize that good results could come from it. For example, Paul said his thorn in the flesh kept him humble. It reminded him he was an ordinary human being, small and frail, inadequate and not self-sufficient. His thorn also taught him to depend on God's strength in hard times. God told Paul, "My grace is sufficient for you, for my power is made perfect in weakness" (v. 9 NIV). Therefore, Paul said, "I delight in weaknesses, in insults, in hardships, in persecutions, in difficulties. For when I am weak, then I am strong" (v. 10 NIV). Rather than letting his thorn in the flesh diminish his life, Paul used it as an opportunity to grow personally and spiritually.

If you read all of Paul's letters, you learn that he made a habit of using trials as growth opportunities. Paul even managed to redeem his time in prison. He used his imprisonment to share the gospel with Roman guards, to pray, to grow in his faith, and to write letters of instruction and encouragement to churches that continue to bless us today. In one of his prison letters, Paul said, "I have learned the secret of being content in any and every situation" (Phil. 4:12 NIV). Clearly Paul's ability to use trials as opportunities of growth contributed significantly to his contentment and happiness.

Learning from a POW

Paul's resiliency reminds me of a remarkable Scottish man named Ernest Gordon. Like Paul, Gordon used severe hardship, including imprisonment, as an opportunity for personal and spiritual growth. During World War II, Japanese soldiers captured Gordon and placed him in a POW camp for four years. He tells his story in his book *Through the Valley of the Kwai,* which inspired the 2001 movie *To End All Wars.*

Gordon faced brutal conditions at the POW camp. Torture, beatings, murder, hunger, slave labor, and disease pervaded the camp. But Gordon and his comrades decided to make the best of their circumstances. They could have given up and died; many did. Or they could have become consumed with bitterness and hatred. Instead, even in that horrible place, they decided to live life as fully as possible.

First Gordon and his friends built a church. Since they had no lumber, they used bamboo. The church reminded them that, even in that desolate place, God was with them. Gordon's experience at the camp had a profound spiritual impact on him. After the war he became a minister and eventually served as dean of the chapel at Princeton University.

Not only did Gordon and his comrades build a church, but they also created a "Jungle University." Although frail in body, their minds were very much alive. So, in the midst of death, disease, slave labor, and abuse, these men created a place of higher learning. They chose to transcend their environment by seeking new understanding and knowledge. Eventually their Jungle University offered courses in history, philosophy, economics, mathematics, literature, ethics, and nine different languages. They even managed to put together a modest library. Gordon and his comrades in the POW camp also studied the arts. They carved wood, sketched pictures, painted, and danced. They studied music as well. A group of the POWs even put together an orchestra made out of bamboo instruments. Another group started up a choir, and several others formed a theater group that presented Shakespearean plays.

Gordon and his fellow POWs found themselves in the most awful circumstances imaginable. And yet in that hellhole they created a Jungle University. Instead of merely surviving, they chose to thrive. As a result they experienced dignity and hope and even a measure of contentment and joy in a brutal POW camp.

Both the apostle Paul and Ernest Gordon took the hardest trials of their life and used them for great personal and spiritual growth. We would do well to follow their example. If we will, both science and Scripture agree that our lives will be happier, more content, and more meaningful.

Inspired by Friends

Through the years I've been blessed with many parishioners and friends who live out the resilient spirit seen in the apostle Paul and Ernest Gordon. Their ability to use trials as growth opportunities constantly inspires me. I'd like to tell you about three of them.

Years ago my dear friend Louise lost her hearing. Although she grieved her loss, she refused to let deafness define her life. Instead she became proficient in lip reading. Then she became an advocate for hearing-impaired persons. For example, she helped bring a unique telephone service for deaf people to her home state of Arkansas. Thousands of lives have been positively impacted by her passion and service. Louise even won a Governor's Award for her tireless efforts on behalf of hearing-impaired persons. In spite of her hearing loss, and in spite of many other challenges in her life including the death of a child, Louise exudes vibrancy and joy. Using her trials as opportunities of growth has brought Louise much contentment and happiness.

At one of my previous pastorates, I met a couple named Harold and Sissy. Their son committed suicide when he was twenty-nine years old. As you would expect, their son's death devastated them. However, that awful experience gave Harold and Sissy a profound empathy and compassion for grieving people. When someone loses a loved one in their church or community, especially if it's a child, Harold and Sissy reach out to them with compassion and wisdom. On several occasions I've seen them become agents of God's grace, strength, and hope for hurting people. Harold and Sissy took the greatest trial of their life and turned it into a ministry for others. By helping other people get through their grief, they found healing for their own grief. In the process Harold and Sissy rediscovered joy and happiness in their lives.

I first met Dr. E. Glenn Hinson when I went to seminary. However, Dr. Hinson had a profound impact on my life even before I met him. During my days as a life insurance agent, I read his book *A Serious Call to a Contemplative Lifestyle*. God used that book, along with other things, to lead me to seminary. After I arrived at seminary, Dr. Hinson continued to bless my life through his classes and books. Dr. Hinson is a brilliant man. He holds two earned doctorates, one in church history and another in theology. He's also fluent in Greek, Latin, and Hebrew. But like the apostle Paul, Dr. Hinson has a "thorn in the flesh." Early in his career he pushed himself beyond human endurance. It resulted in a stroke that impacted his body in many negative ways, including his hearing and speech ability. And yet his health problems made him who he is today—a keenly spiritual man of prayer who has touched the lives of thousands of ministers and tens of thousands of laypeople. Dr. Hinson took a great trial in his life and used it as an opportunity for personal and spiritual growth. As a result, he knows deep contentment in his soul.

If space permitted, I could tell dozens of these kinds of stories. For example, I could tell you about my friend Johnny who has battled colon cancer for years but still pressed on with courage and joy. I could tell you about Craig who lost his leg in a shark attack but used that experience to become an even better person than he was before. I could tell you about Tracy who died several years ago from Lou Gehrig's disease but who lived fully and beautifully until the day he died. The bottom line of all these stories is the same—happy people use trials as growth opportunities.

Getting Started

Hopefully, the above scientific research, scriptural teachings, and real-life examples will inspire you to use the trials in your life as opportunities for growth. If so, the following steps can help you get started.

1. Determine your readiness. Redeeming difficult circumstances is essential for living a contented life. However, you must be emotionally ready before embarking on this journey. For example, if you have recently experienced a significant loss, such as the death of a loved one, a divorce, or a serious medical problem, you must give yourself plenty of time to grieve your loss before moving forward. Then, when you are ready, you can take the next step.

2. Choose to grow. Using trials as growth opportunities rarely happens by accident. For example, I know a man who has been married and divorced four times. To this day he has yet to make the decision to grow from his marital failures. Instead it's always his ex-wife's fault. Until he is ready to take personal responsibility for his own self-growth, he will not make progress. Redeeming painful circumstances takes courage, brutal honesty, intentional self-awareness, and a lot of sweat equity. In order for growth to happen, you must make an intentional choice to walk in that direction, regardless of the challenges.

3. *Learn from others.* As you seek to grow from adversity, learn from others who have already walked that path. Are you recovering from cancer? Seek out a cancer survivor and listen to his or her story. Are you going through a divorce? Talk to someone who survived and then thrived after a failed marriage. Are you dealing with a family member who struggles with substance abuse? Attend local Al-Anon meetings. You can also read articles and books by people who successfully overcame hardships. For example, you might want to read Ernest Gordon's book *To End All Wars*, or Rabbi Kushner's classic *When Bad Things Happen to Good People*.

4. *Seek support.* Although some people can make this growth journey on their own, most of us need others' help. Seek insight and encouragement from family members and friends in your efforts to grow from life's trials. Talk to your pastor and seek his or her guidance, insight, and support. You might even want to schedule several appointments with a professional counselor. It likely will be the best money you have ever spent. As the Bible says, "Two are better than one" (Eccl. 4:9). The insights and encouragement you gain from others will help you better attain your goal of using past and current struggles for personal growth.

5. *Record your progress.* For maximum effectiveness keep a written record of your efforts, both successes and setbacks. As you will see throughout this book, I'm a huge proponent

of journaling. I call it "therapy you can afford." For example, I once challenged a recently divorced member of my congregation to keep a "divorce journal." At first his entries expressed rage and bitterness toward his ex-wife. A few weeks later his entries shifted from anger to deep feelings of grief and loss. A month later he identified and wrote down his own contributions to the failed relationship. Instead of blaming his ex-wife for everything, he realized that he had also contributed to the divorce. Most important, he recorded life lessons from his divorce and recovery that he wanted to remember. Six months later he told me that keeping a divorce journal was the most life-giving, growing experience of his life. Several years later he remarried and stayed married. He attributes his successful second marriage to the growth he experienced while keeping his divorce journal. In fact, he keeps a journal to this day.

6. Celebrate your successes. I'm not recommending that you throw a "I successfully used my trials as a growth opportunity" party! But nonetheless, you need to celebrate your successes along the way. For example, you might want to share some of the fruits of your labor with a friend or family member. Celebrating your success might be as simple as offering God a prayer of gratitude for your recent growth. You can also celebrate your growth successes in a journal. Recording the lessons you've learned from your trials will serve you well, both now and in the future.

"Pick the Fruit and Burn the Rest"

Before concluding this chapter, I want to share with you on a personal, experiential level. Like most people, I've had my share of trials. For example, I constantly struggle with a painful, decades-long throat disorder that consistently threatens my vocation as a minister. Along with the apostle

Paul, I also have a "thorn in the flesh." But thankfully, like Paul, my physical ailment has taught me important lessons, including humility, empathy, setting limits on my schedule, and practicing self-care disciplines.

One of the hardest trials of my life was the loss of my career in my old denomination. I enjoyed an incredibly good situation in that church. I pastored large and interesting congregations, including one in Honolulu, Hawaii. I also worked at the denominational headquarters, taught at a seminary, led clergy workshops across the country, and published many books and articles with my old denomination's publishing house. It was a great ride while it lasted. But then it all collapsed. The leaders of my old denomination moved the church in a fundamentalist direction that I could not and would not support. Therefore, as a matter of personal and theological integrity, I left that denomination in June 1994. However, making that decision proved extremely painful. For a long time, I felt absolutely lost. I struggled with deep feelings of grief, anger, and bitterness. I also spent a lot of time worrying about my future and feeling sorry for myself.

During that difficult time I heard an Episcopal priest named John Claypool, now deceased, tell a story about his grandfather that profoundly impacted my life. For decades a beautiful plum tree stood in the backyard of John Claypool's grandfather's house. The tree was the prize of the farm and the pride of John's grandfather. Then one day a tornado swept through the community. The storm destroyed many trees, including that plum tree. The violent winds ripped the tree from its roots and left it lying lifeless on its side. After the tornado blew over, people ventured outside to survey the damage. Before long a few neighborhood men gathered in John Claypool's grandfather's yard. They stood in a silent circle, gazing down at the once beautiful plum tree, now ruined beyond repair. Finally, one of the men asked John's granddaddy, "What are you going to do with that tree?" After a long pause the old man replied, "I'm going to pick the fruit and burn the rest."

John Claypool, who survived many trials of his own (including the death of his daughter, a divorce, and the loss of his career in the same denomination I left), went on to say that "picking the fruit and burning the rest" is the best response we can make to life's wounds, storms, and losses. First we need to pick the fruit from the struggle, including new sensitivities, insights, and discoveries. Then we need to burn the rest, including any anger, grief, or bitterness. Finally, said Claypool, we need to move forward with our life.

That story was an epiphany for me. It felt like a direct message from God. I knew John Claypool was right. I needed to pick the fruit, burn the rest, and then move forward with my life. So over the next several months that's what I did.

First, I "picked the fruit." And there was much to pick. My old denomination gave me many wonderful gifts for which I'll always be grateful. They introduced me to Jesus, they loved and affirmed me, they became the family for me that my family of origin could not be, they educated me, and they gave me wonderful opportunities of service at a young age. I picked that fruit and will carry it until I die. And there was even more fruit to be picked. The loss of my old career, painful as it was, resulted in significant growth for me. For example, it taught me to let go of the illusion that I am in total control of my life. It also helped teach me humility. Most important, it taught me that my career is not ultimate—only God is. In short, that trial, hard as it was, made me a far better person and pastor.

After picking the fruit, I moved on to "burn the rest." After many years of frustration and grief over the demise of my old denomination, I desperately needed to burn my disappointment, anger, and bitterness and let it go. It took several bonfires to burn away all the old anger and grief, but eventually I did.

Finally, it was time to "move forward with my life." Part of moving forward was finding a new denominational home. The next year I joined the United Methodist Church, a denomination of "Open Hearts, Open Minds, and Open Doors." I felt like I was coming home. The years since that difficult time have been the best years of my life. By picking the fruit, burning the rest, and moving forward with life, I became a far happier and more contented person than I ever was before. I would not trade that experience, painful as it was, for anything.

I tell this story not to talk about my experience but to speak to *your* experience. Most readers of this book are either facing a current trial, recently faced one, or will face one in the near future. It could be an illness, a divorce, a lost job, the death of a loved one, or one of hundreds of other hardships. Unfortunately, ample trials exist to go around. However painful your trial was or is, I encourage you to "pick the fruit" from it. Use your struggle as an opportunity to grow and mature and become stronger and wiser. After you pick the fruit, I encourage you to "burn the rest." Burn the grief, anger, and disappointment, and let it go. If necessary, see your pastor or a professional counselor to help you in this process. Finally, with God's help, I encourage you to "move forward with your life" with courage, hope, and anticipation.

If you will follow John Claypool's advice to "pick the fruit, burn the rest, and move forward with your life," you will undoubtedly become a happier person. You will also become a better person. May that be true in your life and in mine. Amen!

CHAPTER 3

CONTENTED PEOPLE
CULTIVATE OPTIMISM

*Finally, brothers and sisters, whatever is true, whatever is noble,
whatever is right, whatever is pure, whatever is lovely, whatever is
admirable—if anything is excellent or praiseworthy—think about
such things.*

—Philippians 4:8 NIV

I once heard a story about a little boy who worked constantly to maintain a great attitude. No matter what, he
always found a way to cultivate optimism and practice positive thinking. For example, one afternoon he went outside
to his backyard, toting a ball and bat. He said to himself, "I
am the greatest batter in the world!" Then he tossed the ball
into the air, swung at it, and missed. "Strike one!" he yelled.
Undaunted, he picked up the ball and said again, "I'm the
greatest batter in the world!" He tossed the ball into the air.
When it came down, he swung again and missed. "Strike
two!" he cried. He paused a moment to examine his bat and
ball. He spit on his hands and rubbed them together. He
straightened his cap and said once more, "I'm the greatest

batter in the world!" Again he tossed the ball into the air and swung at it. He missed. "Strike three!" Without missing a beat he grinned from ear to ear and shouted, "I'm the greatest *pitcher* in the world!"

In recent years the field of positive psychology has identified numerous traits that lead to contentment. One of them is the practice of cultivating optimism. In other words, contented people foster a positive attitude. They see the glass as half full rather than half empty. However, before diving into this topic, two brief disclaimers need to be noted. First, cultivating optimism is not a major topic in the Bible. Although it's certainly mentioned in Scripture, it's a minor chord, not a major chord. Second, while positive thinking can help depressed persons, this chapter is not about clinical depression. If you think you may suffer from clinical depression, you need to see a doctor for a thorough evaluation. With those two disclaimers we can now move forward.

A Tale of Two Preachers

I often work with new United Methodist clergy in the state of Tennessee. After they graduate from seminary and are appointed to their first full-time church, I help mentor them during their crucial first three years of ministry. Some years ago I worked with a new pastor I'll call Mike. Mike had just been appointed to a small rural church in middle Tennessee. From day one Mike fostered a totally negative attitude about his appointment. He said the church was unfriendly and that the community was backward. He hated the parsonage. He accused the congregation of refusing to make needed changes. According to Mike, everything about this little church was terrible. As you might expect, Mike didn't last long in that appointment. A year later, at Mike's request and at the request of his church, the bishop moved him to another congregation.

A few weeks after Mike moved, the board of ordained ministry asked me to mentor the new pastor at the same church. I'll call him Sam. From day one Sam expressed positive feelings about his appointment. He loved the congregation, the community, and the parsonage. He told me the congregation cooperated fully with his ideas and suggestions. Sam spent four wonderful years at that church before being appointed to a larger congregation.

I've thought a lot about that experience. Both men went to the same church. Both were young. Both had just graduated from seminary. Both had similar theology. And both were competent ministers. But they had radically different experiences. The reason they had radically different experiences is because they had dramatically different attitudes. Mike fostered a negative attitude at the church, failed miserably, and felt terribly unhappy there. Sam cultivated an optimistic attitude at the church, succeeded greatly, and felt extremely happy in the appointment. Their attitude made all the difference.

The Science of Optimism

Positive psychologists would not be surprised by the story of Mike and Sam. For example, Martin Seligman, a psychologist and happiness expert, often asks people to practice an exercise called "What-Went-Well." It's also called "Three Blessings." Seligman believes people think too much about what goes wrong in their lives and not enough about what goes well. So he often encourages people to spend ten minutes a day identifying and writing down three things that went well that day and why they went well. He discovered that the results of this exercise can be dramatic.

For example, back in 2005, *Time* magazine ran a cover story on positive psychology and mentioned Seligman's work in the field. Anticipating a huge response, his team opened a website offering one free exercise—the "what-went-well" activity mentioned above. Many thousands of people registered on the site. Seligman and his team were able to identify the fifty most depressed people who registered on the site who took the depression and happiness tests and who also did the "what-went-well" exercise. This group had an average depression score of 34, which means they were extremely depressed, making it a struggle to carry out simple daily functions. Each of them participated in the "what-went-well" exercise every day for one week. Then they reported back to the website. On average their depression score dropped from 34 to 17, a huge decrease. That moved them from "extreme" depression to the cusp of "mild-moderate" depression. Perhaps even more impressive, their happiness score jumped from the fifteenth percentile to the fiftieth percentile. By focusing on the positives in their lives instead of the negatives, forty-seven out of the fifty were, in short order, less depressed and happier.[1]

Another example of the power of positive thinking can be found in Seligman's book *Authentic Happiness*. In this book Seligman cites a long-term study of a group of Roman Catholic nuns. In a nutshell the study revealed that the nuns who cultivated optimism lived significantly longer than those who did not. The study discovered that 90 percent of the most cheerful quarter of the nuns in the study were alive at age eight-five versus only 34 percent of the least cheerful quarter; 54 percent of the most cheerful quarter were alive at age ninety-four, as opposed to 11 percent of the least cheerful quarter. Seligman concludes from the study that "a happy nun is a long-lived nun."[2] Other happiness experts come to the same conclusion. Fostering a positive attitude reaps major beneficial results, including reducing depression, enhancing work performance, strengthening family life and other relationships, improving physical health, and extending life span.

Cultivating optimism, however, does not mean a person ignores pain, suffering, and difficult challenges. That's not real, and it's counterproductive to enhancing true contentment. Happy people don't ignore reality. However, they do choose to focus more on the positives than on the negatives, as the following story vividly illustrates.

"You Must Think about What You Have Left"

Many of you are familiar with Bob Dole, a member of "the greatest generation." Not long ago I read his inspiring autobiography, *One Soldier's Story*. Bob grew up in Russell, Kansas. In the heartland of America, Bob learned to work hard, depend on family, trust God, love and serve his country, and foster a "can-do" positive attitude.

In his early years Bob excelled as an athlete. He ran track and played football and basketball, including college ball. However, while Bob was attending college, Japan attacked Pearl Harbor, and the United States went to war. Like so many other American young men in those days, Bob enlisted. The military sent him to officer training school, made him a first lieutenant, and then shipped him off to war. And then, in April 1945, just days before the war concluded, while leading his men up a hill in Italy, enemy forces brutally shot Lt. Bob Dole. Bob almost died that day, and he almost died several other times as a result of his horrible injuries. He spent three years in hospitals trying to recover. Paralyzed at first, he slowly regained the use of his legs, although they never worked as well again. He never regained full use of his arms and hands.

During those first few months, Bob experienced times of self-pity and bitterness, but he refused to focus on the negatives. Instead he continued to believe that he still had a viable future. One day the doctor told Bob the hard truth. There would be no miracles. They could do surgery, probably several surgeries, but he would always be disabled. He might get back 30 to 40 percent of the use of his right arm, but it would never be the same. His shoulder would never rotate. He would never be able to lift his arm above his head. He would not run much, and he would certainly not play basketball again. However, he would partially recover, and then he would have to make the best of his physical limitations. Bob said to the doctor: "Well, what do we do? Where do we start?" Dr. Kelikian leaned forward in his chair, his eyes glued to Bob's, and said: "We start by not thinking so much anymore about what you have lost. You must think about what you have left . . . and what you can do with it."[3]

Bob said that although that doctor did not perform a medical miracle on him, he performed a different kind of miracle. "He inspired within me a new attitude, a new way of looking at my life, urging me to focus on what I had left and what I could do with it, rather than complaining about what had been lost and could never be repaired. He encouraged me to see possibilities where others saw only problems. It's an attitude that has served me well over the years, and I will always be grateful to Dr. K."[4]

As many of you know, Bob took his doctor's advice. He rejected the path of bitterness and negativity. Instead he chose the path of optimism and positive thinking. Bob went back to college and then to law school. He married and eventually went on to have a remarkable and distinguished career as a U.S. senator. Bob Dole experienced significant losses in his life. And like anyone else he had moments of despair and bitterness. But Bob choose to focus on the good things in his life rather than the bad, which blessed not only him and his family but also our entire country.

Another Tale of Two Preachers

Numerous examples of the power of attitude—positive or negative—can be found in Scripture. For example, Proverbs 17:22 says, "A cheerful heart is a good medicine, but a downcast spirit dries up the bones." The Bible clearly teaches the value of cultivating optimism, as we can see in the following stories about two preachers—the Old Testament prophet Elijah and the New Testament apostle Paul.

First Kings 19 tells a fascinating story about the prophet Elijah. The story begins with Elijah in the wilderness, discouraged, depressed, and burned out, ready to throw in the towel. In despair Elijah asked God to let him die. He said, "It is enough; now, O LORD, take away my life, for I am no better than my ancestors" (v. 4). Numerous factors played into Elijah's feelings of despair, including negative thinking. In the story Elijah said to God, "I have been very zealous for the LORD, the God of hosts; for the Israelites have forsaken your covenant, thrown down your altars, and killed your prophets with the sword. I alone am left, and they are seeking my life, to take it away" (v. 10).

Elijah basically said, "Lord, I'm the only faithful person left in all of Israel. All the other people have compromised their faith. Nobody else has been diligent in serving you. I am the only faithful believer left in the entire country." Talk about negative thinking! Elijah's view was far too pessimistic. He wasn't the only faithful person left, not by a long shot. This kind of pessimistic attitude is one of the major reasons Elijah got burned out and discouraged in the first place. Elijah's perspective proved far too negative an assessment.

God responded, "I will leave seven thousand in Israel, all the knees that have not bowed to Baal, and every mouth that has not kissed him" (v. 18). God said, "Elijah, your math is off by 6,999! Thousands of faithful people are left — you are not the only one." In a nutshell God said, "Elijah, you are being far too negative. You need to adjust your attitude." Thankfully Elijah eventually recovered. His journey toward wholeness involved numerous steps, including an attitude adjustment. When he became more optimistic, he took a major step toward wholeness. If you and I want to get well and stay well, we, like Elijah, must decrease our negative thinking and increase our positive thinking, as we see in the following example of another biblical preacher.

In his letter to the Philippians, the apostle Paul said, "Finally, beloved, whatever is true, whatever is honorable, whatever is just, whatever is pure, whatever is pleasing, whatever is commendable, if there is any excellence and if there is anything worthy of praise, think about these things" (4:8). You may be aware that Paul wrote those words while in prison. Even in difficult circumstances Paul encouraged his readers to focus on the good and to choose a positive attitude. Throughout the book of Philippians and in his other letters, Paul consistently cultivated optimism. Rather than focusing on his problems, he focused on the good. Paul's attitude provides at least two principles for us.

First, *fostering optimism is an act of discipline.* Paul worked hard to cultivate a positive spirit. Paul could easily have focused on the negatives. He was in prison, problems abounded in his churches, and he suffered from a serious physical ailment. Paul noted his trials in his letters; he honestly expressed the challenges he faced. Yet in his letter to the Philippians and in his other letters, Paul overflowed with optimism. Instead of dwelling on problems, he constantly focused on the good things that were happening. Paul said, "Yes, I'm in prison, but I'm using it as an opportunity to share the gospel with the Roman authorities. Yes, I have a physical problem, a 'thorn in the flesh,' but it's teaching me humility and making me depend on God's strength and not just my own strength. Yes, I face many challenges, but God is with me, my friends are supporting me and praying for me, and that is enough." Paul clearly *worked* at being positive. Cultivating optimism is an act of discipline—it takes effort and work and practice.

Second, *cultivating optimism is an act of faith.* Paul was no Pollyanna. He knew about pain and suffering. Paul's admonition about focusing on the good was not an exercise in shallow positive-thinking philosophy. Paul's ability to foster a positive and optimistic attitude grew out of his faith. He expressed optimism because he knew God was with him and because he knew God actively worked in the world. In short, Paul's optimism was rooted in his faith, especially his faith in the resurrection of Jesus Christ. If God can raise Jesus from the dead, any situation has hope, including death itself. So Paul's optimism came from his faith—faith in a living, resurrected God who gives hope to every circumstance.

Ultimately we, like Paul, have to make a choice in life. Will we focus on the negatives? Or will we focus on the positives? Life will always bring good and bad, so we must choose where to place our focus. Paul chose to focus on the positives.

Things I Have Not Lost

Some years ago I experienced overwhelming losses. It proved the most difficult experience of my life. I felt brutalized by pain and grief, and I wondered if I would ever fully recover. About that time I happened to read a brief article by Michael J. Fox. As some of you know, Michael J. Fox enjoyed a remarkably successful career as an actor both in television and on the big screen, including his hit television show *Family Ties* and his popular *Back to the Future* trilogy of movies. He currently plays a character in the popular television show *The Good Wife*. However, years ago Michael developed Parkinson's disease, a debilitating illness. In his article he spoke briefly about the loss of his health. But then he went on to speak about all the things he had *not* lost, including his family, his friends, and his zest for living and working. The article proved an epiphany experience for me.

The next evening I blocked out an hour at my home office to write in my journal. In that entry I poured out the deep losses, pain, anger, and grief that I felt. I held nothing back. I wrote a ruthlessly honest expression of my wounds. I then paused, thought about Michael J. Fox's article, turned the page, and wrote in large caps: "THINGS I HAVE NOT LOST." For the next thirty minutes, I wrote like a madman. I listed all the good things in my life I could think of that had not been lost. For example, I wrote:

- I have not lost my marriage.
- I have not lost my children.
- I have not lost my friends.
- I have not lost my health.
- I have not lost my faith.
- I have not lost my vocation.
- I have not lost my hope.

By the time I finished, I had listed over fifteen major things in my life that I had not lost. Under each heading I wrote several sentences to several paragraphs, fleshing out the main point I had just written down. For example, after writing, "I have not lost my marriage," I noted that I had not lost my wife of many years who loved, accepted, and supported me through good and bad. I wrote all the things

I appreciated about her and how much she had blessed my life. Then I went to the next major point, listing another blessing I had not lost and again filling in the details. This went on page after page until my hand ached from writing.

That journal entry became the turning point in my recovery. For the next several weeks, I daily reread that entry. I also continued to write about every positive thing in my life I could think of, both big and small—regardless of the major losses I had experienced. Within a few months my contentment level returned to where it had been before the losses. Through that experience I learned the power of following Paul's admission, "Finally, beloved, whatever is true, whatever is honorable, whatever is just, whatever is pure, whatever is pleasing, whatever is commendable, if there is any excellence and if there is anything worthy of praise, think about these things" (Phil. 4:8). Much more could be said about cultivating optimism. If you want to pursue this further, I recommend you read the sections on fostering greater optimism in Sonja Lyubomirsky's *The How of Happiness* and Martin Seligman's *Authentic Happiness*.

Through the years I've personally experienced the life-giving power of fostering a positive attitude, and I've seen hundreds of others do the same in my work as a pastor. The best practical advice I can offer to help in this effort is to spend time, at least several days a week, writing down the good things happening in your life, large and small, from your primary relationships to a funny joke that made you laugh. It takes only a few minutes. But the benefits are profound and lasting.

Cutting Stones and Building Cathedrals

I'll end this chapter by telling you one of my favorite stories. It comes from the fourteenth century. I don't know if the story is literally true or not. It's probably a legend or a parable. But regardless, the story is full of great truth.

One day, way back in fourteenth-century France, a priest talked with three stonecutters working on a cathedral. When the priest asked the first stonecutter what he was doing, the stonecutter bitterly told him that he was cutting stones into blocks, one foot by one foot by three quarters of a foot. In frustration the stonecutter described a miserable life in which he cut stones over and over and over again, adding that he would have to do so until the day he died. This stonecutter was definitely not cultivating optimism! He had not read Philippians 4, or if he had, he chose not to obey it.

The priest then walked a little farther and asked a second stonecutter what he was doing. The second man, also cutting stones into blocks, replied in a different way. When asked what he was doing, he warmly replied that he was earning a respectable living. Because of his employment he could take care of his family. Cutting stones allowed his children to have clothes to wear, food to eat, and a decent house to live in. He and his wife had a modest but nice home, which they filled with love, all because he was cutting stone into blocks. Quite a different attitude from the first stonecutter.

Finally, the priest walked a little farther and asked a third stonecutter what he was doing. In a joyous voice he said, "I'm helping build a great cathedral to the glory of God, a cathedral that will stand for over a thousand years that will be an inspiration to all who see it!"

What a remarkable story. Three men doing the same job. But what a difference in attitude! One man cut stones in boredom and misery. One man cut stones to care for his family. And one man cut stones for the glory of God. Imagine that.

CHAPTER 4

CONTENTED PEOPLE
FOCUS ON THE PRESENT

So don't be anxious about tomorrow. God will take care of your tomorrow too. Live one day at a time.

— Matthew 6:34 TLB

The *New Yorker* once published a humorous yet insightful cartoon. The cartoon included three panels. In the first panel a man sits at his desk in his office, daydreaming about playing golf. The next panel depicts the same man on the golf course. However, instead of focusing on his golf game, he fantasizes about being with a woman. The final panel finds the man with the woman he fantasized about. However, rather than savoring his moment with the woman, he's thinking about work! Like the man in the cartoon, many Americans fail to fully enjoy the present moment. Instead our minds are often someplace else, usually in the past or the future.

Over a hundred years ago, Maurice Maeterlinck wrote a play called *The Blue Bird.* In the play a fairy tells two children a story about the bluebird of happiness. She then sends them on a quest to find the bluebird. After a year of searching and many adventures, the children finally come back. But their journey proved unsuccessful. In spite of looking in many places, they could not find the bluebird of happiness. However, when they arrive home, they find the bluebird waiting for them. One of the children says, "It's the bluebird we were looking for! We've been miles and miles and miles, and he was here all the time!"

Like those children in the fairy tale, contented people don't find happiness in far-off and exotic places. Instead they find contentment in their current circumstances in the present moment. Like Dorothy in *The Wizard of Oz*, they finally learn the lesson "that if I ever go looking for my heart's desire again, I won't look any further than my own backyard. Because if it isn't there, I never really lost it to begin with."

Living in the Present: Insights from Science

As we've already noted, positive psychologists have discovered numerous traits that lead to happiness. One of their findings is that contented people focus on the present moment. That doesn't mean they forget the past or neglect the future. But they put their primary attention on living in the present.

Unfortunately a lot of people don't do that. Some get stuck in the past, ruminating on successes or failures of years gone by. Others stay overly focused on the future. They think to themselves: *When I get out of school, or when I get married, or when I have kids, or when the kids leave home, or when I get a promotion, or when I get my dream house, or when I retire from my job, then my life will be good.* All the while they neglect the present moment, and before they know it, their life is over. So psychologists tell us—if we want to be happy and content, we must learn to live right here, right now, focused on the present moment.

For example, happiness expert Seligman says, "The sheer speed of modern life and our extreme future-mindedness can sneak up on us and impoverish our present." He notes that by rushing through the current moment and obsessing over the future, "we lose acres of the present."[1]

Learning to live in the present moment takes discipline, effort, and practice. Psychologists use terms like *flow*, *mindfulness*, and *savoring* to explain this important behavior. In a nutshell it's an effort to fully engage and fully appreciate the present moment. For specific strategies about how to do this, you can read positive psychology resources like *Authentic Happiness* and *The How of Happiness*.[2] For our purposes in this book, it's enough to say that psychological research confirms that happy people, while not neglecting the past and the future, consistently focus on the present moment.

Living in the Present: Insights from Scripture

Once again, when it comes to finding life satisfaction, science and Scripture concur. The Bible clearly teaches us to focus on the present moment. Many examples could be given. For example, during my teenage years my youth group went to a pizza joint every Sunday night after church. On the wall of the pizza parlor hung a huge poster of a child sitting in a high chair. The child, grinning from ear to ear, had just poured a big bowl of spaghetti over his head. The caption said, "This is the day that the LORD has made; let us rejoice and be glad in it" (Ps. 118:24).

The psalmist and other writers of the Bible understood that life is brief. In fact, one biblical writer once prayed, "Teach us to number our days, that we may gain a heart of wisdom" (Ps. 90:12 NIV). When we realize that life is short, we won't waste it by dwelling too much on the past or the future. Instead, we will learn to live today, in the present moment, because that's really all we have. We can't change yesterday. We don't know about tomorrow. What we do have is *today*. We certainly can't ignore the past and future, for they are important. But we should not *dwell* there. Instead, God tells us to focus on today. Thus the psalmist says, "This is the day that the LORD has made; let us rejoice and be glad in it." Even with the pain, stress, and struggles of life, God wants us to savor, rejoice, and be glad in the gifts of the day. In short, God calls us to live fully in the present.

We see the same theme in the teachings of Jesus. For example, in Matthew 6, Jesus warns us not to be overly anxious about the future. He tells us not to worry too much about what we will eat, drink, or wear, for we don't know what tomorrow will bring. Therefore, worrying about the future is futile. Instead Jesus encourages us to live in the present moment. In this text Jesus said, "So do not worry about tomorrow, for tomorrow will bring worries of its own. Today's trouble is enough for today" (Matt. 6:34). *The Living Bible* paraphrase of this passage helps capture the intent of Jesus' words. It says, "So don't be anxious about tomorrow. God will take care of your tomorrow too. Live one day at a time."

One of my favorite passages in the Bible is Jeremiah 29. Back when Jeremiah wrote these words, the people of Israel lived in exile in Babylon. Unhappy and homesick, they constantly reminisced about the good old days in Jerusalem and fantasized about returning home. In short they spent their time living in the past and in the future but not in the present. In that setting, God sent a message to the exiles through a letter written by the prophet Jeremiah. In that letter Jeremiah said: "This is what the LORD Almighty, the God of

Israel, says to all those I carried into exile from Jerusalem to Babylon: 'Build houses and settle down; plant gardens and eat what they produce. Marry and have sons and daughters; find wives for your sons and give your daughters in marriage, so that they too may have sons and daughters. Increase in numbers there; do not decrease. Also, seek the peace and prosperity of the city to which I have carried you into exile. Pray to the LORD for it, because if it prospers, you too will prosper" (Jer. 29:4–7 NIV).

In this letter, God told the people of Israel to stop focusing on the past and the future and start living in the present moment, right where they were in Babylon. We would do well to follow that same advice.

Like the psalmist, Jesus, and Jeremiah, the writer of Ecclesiastes understood the importance of living in the present moment, and he wrote about it in his book. However, in keeping with his overall cynical tone, the Teacher of Ecclesiastes began on a negative note before moving to a positive one. In chapter 9 he said, "This is an evil in all that happens under the sun, that the same fate comes to everyone. . . . The living know that they will die. . . . Never again will they have any share in all that happens under the sun" (Eccl. 9:3, 5–6). When I read this text to my congregation a few months ago, I said: "This is such a heartwarming passage of Scripture. I think you should post it on your bathroom mirror and read it every morning for inspiration!"

Thankfully, on a more positive note, Ecclesiastes finally realized that life is short and we'd better enjoy the journey while we still have time. So right after saying we are all going to die, he immediately added, "Go, eat your bread with enjoyment, and drink your wine with a merry heart; for God has long ago approved what you do" (9:7).

In this passage the writer of Ecclesiastes tells us that one of the keys to living a contented life is to enjoy the journey and to do so now, before our time is gone. Thankfully,

Ecclesiastes doesn't just tell us to enjoy the journey—he also gives us four practical suggestions for doing so.

The Teacher of Ecclesiastes first suggests that to enjoy the journey we need to *appreciate the simple gifts*. He says, "Go, eat your bread with enjoyment, and drink your wine with a merry heart" (Eccl. 9:7). If we want to experience contentment on the journey, we must appreciate the simple joys of living, for example, lunch with a friend; a beautiful sunset; an engaging novel; a creative movie; a walk in the park; the beauty of spring; a game of catch with our kids; intimacy with our spouse; dinner around the table with family or friends; grandchildren coming to our house; grandchildren leaving our house; a beautiful song; a funny joke; or a tall glass of strong, sweet, southern iced tea. To truly live we must appreciate the simple gifts of life.

Ecclesiastes' second suggestion for enjoying the journey is to *remember to celebrate*. In this text the writer says, "Let your garments always be white; do not let oil be lacking on your head" (Eccl. 9:8). White garments and oil were ancient symbols of festivity and celebration. Ecclesiastes is telling us to celebrate life, to have some fun, to have a party or two. That's the advice I once heard from a doctor. He said, "I've done the research, and I hate to tell you, but everybody dies—lovers, joggers, vegetarians, and nonsmokers. I'm telling you this so that some of you who jog at 5:00 a.m. and eat vegetables will occasionally sleep late and have an ice cream cone." Inspired by these words, I went out and bought not one but two quarts of Baskin-Robbins ice cream!

Ecclesiastes' third suggestion for enjoying the journey is to *enjoy our relationships*. He said, "Enjoy life with the wife whom you love" (Eccl. 9:9). We all know that relationships can sometimes be complicated, strained, and painful. But other than our faith, the people in our lives are the most important part of our existence. So Ecclesiastes encourages us to enjoy our relationships—with our spouse if we are married—but also with other family members, friends, coworkers, neighbors, and church family.

Ecclesiastes' final suggestion for enjoying the journey is to *work with enthusiasm*. He said, "Whatever your hand finds to do, do with your might" (Eccl. 9:10). Ecclesiastes tells us to throw ourselves into our work with zest and energy. Whether we work at home, at school, at the office, or as a volunteer in our church or community, Ecclesiastes tells us to dive in and work with gusto.

According to Ecclesiastes one of the keys to a well-lived life is enjoying the journey, living fully in the present moment. Of course, that does not mean we won't have trials, struggles, and tears along the way. Of course we will. But in spite of the struggles, God wants us to appreciate and enjoy the incredible gift of being alive. Even in the hard times, God wants us to be grateful for the journey and to enjoy the journey. In short, God calls us to live fully in the present moment.

Ecclesiastes' words about enjoying the journey remind me of an essay by Robert Hastings called "The Station." In his essay Hastings says that most of us are overly fixated on the destinations of life, what he calls "The Station." We think that when we graduate from college, or get a promotion, or lose twenty pounds, or buy that new house, or retire—when we get to the destination ("the station")—then we'll enjoy life and fully live. But Hastings says we've gotten it all wrong. The destination is *not* the point. The *journey* is the point. Hastings says that if we want to have a contented life we must learn how to enjoy the journey, which is exactly what Ecclesiastes is saying in this text. Robert Hastings concludes his essay with these words: "So, stop pacing the aisles and counting the miles. Instead, climb more mountains, eat more ice cream, go barefoot more often, swim more rivers, watch more sunsets, laugh more, cry less. Life must be lived as we go along. The station will come soon enough."[3]

Living in the Present:
Insights from Experience

This concept of living in the present moment became especially relevant to me twenty years ago when I decided to transfer from my old denomination to the United Methodist Church. The year I transferred few pastoral appointments came open. As a result, church officials sent me to a small church in a tiny town. When I first received the news, I felt devastated. After years of serving as a large-church pastor and as a national denominational worker, this felt like a huge demotion. I called an older pastor in the Methodist Church to talk about this development. At first he expressed great disappointment in my appointment. But then he said: "Don't worry about it, Martin. Go to the church, spend one year there, two at the very most, and then move to a bigger church."

After hanging up the phone, I carefully thought about what he said. The more I thought about it, the more I realized— his recommendation was a bankrupt way to live. Right then and there I made a decision, one of the most important decisions of my life. I decided I was not going to live for my next appointment. Instead, I decided to live fully in my *current* appointment, even in that small town and church, totally immersing myself into the congregation and the community.

I could tell you many things about that appointment. However, the most important thing I can say is that the four years I spent there were among the best four years of my entire life. In fact, when the bishop moved me to a new church, I cried my heart out. It's not because the church and town were perfect. The town is a typical small town with plenty of positives and negatives. The same was true with the church. So why was life so good there? There's no question in my mind. Before moving to that small community, I focused almost exclusively on the future. I constantly made long-range plans, was always thinking ahead, and mostly lived for tomorrow. I had even developed a five-, ten-, and twenty-year career plan. Believe me, going to that tiny town and church was not part of the plan! So I threw out my long-range plan and never replaced it. For the first time in my life, I decided to leave the future to God and got busy living in the present moment. I fully invested myself into that church and community. In the words of Jeremiah cited above, I built a home, planted a garden, and sought the welfare of the city—and it transformed my life.

Soon after arriving in that little town, my wife and I connected with a group of folks in the community who became dear friends. Every Sunday night about a dozen of us gathered together to eat and visit. One of our running jokes was that when it comes to money, there are only two kinds of people in the world: people who save for tomorrow and people who live for today. When it comes to money, I'm pretty much a save-for-tomorrow kind of guy. However, my friends in that group were live-for-today kinds of people. Over a period of about four months, virtually every one of our friends bought a new car. When they bought their cars, I razzed them about living for today instead of saving for tomorrow. In fact, I gave them some real grief about it. I joked: "You ought to be saving for tomorrow instead of living for today. You just wait. One day when you retire, you will come to me to take out a loan!"

Several months later, my son graduated from college and needed a car. So I gave him my fully paid-for Toyota Corolla and then went out and bought a brand-new car. Not only did I purchase a new car, but I upgraded. Instead of a Corolla, I bought a Toyota Camry. Our friends had a field day with that. All of a sudden this save-for-tomorrow guy was living for today, and they ribbed me about it without mercy. The next Sunday night, when we gathered for dinner, they made a special presentation on my behalf with several speeches. They even gave me a framed certificate that I still have. It said, "Congratulations to Martin Thielen, the newest member of the 'Living for Today' Club."

I still believe in saving for tomorrow. But while living in that little community, I truly became a member of the "Living for Today Club." Since that experience, I have focused far more on living in the present than living in the past or the future. And my life is far richer for it.

The Best Time of My Life

A few weeks before we left that town, a close friend and member of the group gave me an essay that touched me deeply. I saved it and have read it many times. It's called, "The Best Time of My Life," by Joe Kemp. Joe began his essay by telling about his upcoming thirtieth birthday. Apprehensive about turning thirty, he wondered if the best years of his life might be over. So Joe talked about his concern to one of his friends at the gym, an elderly yet healthy man named Nicholas. Joe asked Nicholas, "What was the best time of your life?" In a remarkable response Nicholas told Joe that when he was a child in Austria and loved by his parents, that was the best time of his life. When he went to school and learned his trade, that was the best time of his life. When he got his first job and began making a living, that was the best time of his life. When he fell in love and married his wife, that was the best time of his life. When he and his wife escaped from Austria during the war and boarded a ship bound for North America, that was the best time of his life. When he and his wife had children and raised them, that was the best time of his life. Then Nicholas told Joe that although he was now seventy-nine years old, he was still healthy and he still deeply loved his wife. He concluded, "This is the best time of my life."[4]

Science, Scripture, and personal experience all point to the same conclusion. Contented people focus on living in the present moment. They know that life's circumstances are never going to be perfect. So instead of chasing around the globe seeking the bluebird of paradise, they make the best out of their current circumstances and live fully in the present moment. And when they do, they eventually come to realize, like the children in the play, that the bluebird of happiness "was here all the time." This truth reminds me of one of my favorite stories. It's called "The Stonecutter."

The Stonecutter

Once upon a time a stonecutter lived in a small village. He earned a modest income and lived a simple life. Although highly skilled in his craft, and deeply respected and loved by the people in his village, he often felt restless and discontent. He often thought, *If only I had a more glamorous job and lived in a more exciting community, then I would be content.*

One day as the stonecutter worked with his hammer and chisel on a huge stone, he heard a noisy crowd gathering along the street. He joined the procession and soon saw what all the excitement was about. The king was passing through their humble village! The stonecutter gazed in awe as the king, dressed in marvelous silk, was greeted by his subjects. *Oh, how I wish I had the power and glory of the king,* he thought. *He rides a magnificent horse. He has soldiers at his command. People bow to him in homage. There is no one more powerful than our king.*

The heavens heard his cry, and immediately the humble stonecutter found himself transformed into a powerful king. He found himself riding on a great horse, waving at crowds of people who flocked to see him. *This is power,* he thought. However, as the summer progressed, the new king watched the effects of the heat on his people. Men and animals became weary, and plants withered under the powerful rays of the sun. As he looked at the sky, the new king realized that the sun was far more powerful than any earthly ruler. *How I wish I were as powerful as that*, he thought. *I wish I were the sun.* Immediately his wish was granted.

He relished his new role as the sun and gloried in his power. As he sent bright rays to the earth, he watched kings and princes hide under their parasols. He watched powerful warriors become weak under his gaze. Even the crops in the field fell under his command. Then one day a large cloud moved over the land, shielding the earth from the sun's bright rays. As hard as he tried, he could not penetrate the cloud. Seeing something more powerful than himself, he thought, *I want to be a cloud.* Again he received his wish.

Now he blocked the sun's rays and felt important. He became a gigantic cloud and began to pour down torrential rain on the earth. Rivers formed where previously there were none, and water flooded the streets of the cities and the farmland. Everything—trees, animals, and people—seemed awed by his power. Everything except a huge rock that remained untouched. Again he had discovered something more powerful. *There is nothing*, he thought, *as powerful as a rock. How I wish I were a huge stone.* Again his wish was granted.

As a massive stone he remained motionless and powerful, unmoved by either sun or rain or anything that nature could bring, making him feel superior over all things. Then one day a man approached him, carrying a bag. When he stopped, he pulled out a chisel and a hammer and began to chip away at the rock. Realizing that the man with the tools was more powerful than any rock, he cried out, "Oh, how I want to be a stonecutter." One final time the heavens heard his cry and granted his wish, and he became a stonecutter. Once again he lived a modest life in a simple village and made his living with a hammer and chisel. And he was content.

CHAPTER 5

CONTENTED PEOPLE
PRACTICE FORGIVENESS

Forgive us our sins, for we also forgive everyone who sins against us.
—Luke 11:4 NIV

I once heard about an East Texas town that decided to put on a community-wide Easter pageant. They chose the biggest and burliest guy in town to play the part of Jesus. He was the only one strong enough to carry the heavy cross all the way through town, up to the hillside, where the crucifixion would take place. Everyone in town called him "Redneck Jesus." The day of the pageant, the townspeople lined the street and began jeering at Redneck Jesus as he made his way through the center of town. One of his friends got a bit carried away. As Redneck Jesus walked by, his friend loudly cursed him, crying out, "Crucify him! Crucify him!" He even spit on him. Redneck Jesus decided that was enough. He shouted out, in a voice that everyone could hear, "You just wait until after the resurrection. I'll get you."

\Most of us can relate. When we are abused, revenge is far more natural and easier than forgiveness. Yet Jesus taught us to forgive. And he didn't just teach it; he modeled it. When the real Jesus carried his cross through town and up the hill to be executed and the people screamed at him and spit on him, he didn't say, "You just wait until after the resurrection. I'll get you." Instead he said, "Father, forgive them, for they do not know what they are doing."

As a minister I've been in the forgiveness business for over thirty years. For decades I've preached forgiveness, taught forgiveness, counseled forgiveness, and practiced forgiveness. I've seen firsthand the life-giving benefits of forgiveness and the tragic consequences of not forgiving. I've learned from Scripture, theology, professional experience, personal experience, and psychological research that if people want to be content, they must obey Jesus' command to practice forgiveness.

Three Stories of Forgiveness

As we begin exploring the subject of forgiveness, I'd like to share three stories from my own experience. First, I'll tell you a story about forgiving my father. Second, I'll share a story about forgiving a church member I detested. Finally, I'll tell you a story about forgiving a man who committed a felony against me.

Forgiving My Father. My father was a good man in many ways. But he was not a good father. He deeply wounded my brother, sister, and me, and we've struggled with those wounds our entire lives. Mostly, my father was an absentee parent. I do not have even one childhood memory of doing something enjoyable with my dad. When he did interact with his children, my father constantly expressed disappointment and condemnation. He also drank a lot, which exasperated his negativity with his three children. For some reason, special occasions like Thanksgiving and Christmas proved especially brutal. Although my father never physically abused me, he emotionally abused me throughout my childhood and youth. In short, my dad miserably failed as a father. However, in his later years, I decided it was past time to forgive my dad, especially after learning about his own loveless and difficult childhood. Through that process of forgiveness, we eventually made peace with each other. When he died back in 1993, I lived in Hawaii, so I had to fly to my parents' home in Arkansas for the funeral.

Two weeks later, before I returned home to Hawaii, I went to his grave for final closure on forgiving him. I had come a long way in my efforts to forgive him, but I still had some unfinished business. As I stood in front of his grave, I verbally told my dad that I forgave him for his failures as a father. I forgave him for his neglect. I forgave him for his hostility and negativity. I forgave him for never affirming me or telling me he loved me. I forgave him for drinking too much. Over and over again, I said, "I forgive you." I wept for a long time after that. Then I told my dad how much I appreciated his many good traits and listed them. For example, my father was honest, hardworking, provided for his family, served his country faithfully as an Air Force pilot, and respected people of all races and religions. After verbally expressing his many good traits, I cried some more. Finally, I left his graveside, got into the car, and drove away. As I left the cemetery, I felt a weight lifted from my soul that never returned. Today when I think about my dad, I no longer feel the old resentment that haunted me for years. Instead I appreciate his many good traits, have long forgiven his failures, and am at peace with him.

Forgiving a Church Member. Years ago when I pastored in another state, a church member devoted his life to making me as miserable as possible. He constantly criticized and condemned me without mercy. A week rarely passed without another assault. He didn't just pick on me; he attacked the entire staff. For example, on many occasions, he brought our church secretaries to tears. He once took our associate pastor golfing. The next day he began telling everyone in town that the associate pastor spent his workdays golfing instead of working. Clearly a miserable man, he took out his unhappiness on everyone around him, including me and our church staff.

I tried to reconcile with him at least a half dozen times, but it never worked. Over the years I grew to hate this man. I felt deep bitterness toward him. Sadly this relationship began to take a serious toll on my spiritual life. Several months later, before moving to a new pastorate, I decided that I did not want to take that bitterness with me to my new congregation. So I began praying every day for God's help to forgive him. The day before we moved, I drove to this man's business. I didn't go in to see him because it would not have done any good. I learned the hard way that directly contacting him only made things worse. So I parked my car in the parking lot of his business, turned off the engine, and began to pray the phrase from the Lord's Prayer that says, "Forgive us our sins as we forgive those who sin against us." Then I called this man's name and said, "I forgive you." A moment later I said it a second time. Then, with a loud voice, I shouted a third time, "I forgive you." As I drove away from the parking lot, I felt liberated. I left my bitterness toward this man on that parking lot, and I've rarely thought of him since.

Forgiving a Felon. Many years ago a man wronged me in a significant way. The details are not important, but he went to prison for what he did. About a year later I decided that I needed, for my own sake, to forgive him. Over the months that followed, I slowly let go of my negative thoughts and feelings toward this man and forgave him. I did this for my benefit, not his, so I made no effort to reach out to him.

Several years later he called me unexpectedly on the phone. The state had recently released him from prison, and he wanted to apologize to me. He told me he had finally gotten his life together, had found God, and needed to apologize and ask for my forgiveness. I accepted his apology and told him that, although I had forgiven him a long time ago, I appreciated his call. Before concluding our conversation, I said: "I wish nothing but good things for you in the future. May God's blessings be with you." With great emotion he thanked me and said he could now move forward in his life.

I've never talked to him again and don't plan to. Just because you forgive someone doesn't mean you have to be friends with them. And my forgiveness certainly did not mean that I condoned his behavior. You can fully forgive someone but still acknowledge that their behavior was wrong and that they must accept the consequences of their actions. Anyway, forgiving this man helped me move forward with my life, and it helped him do the same.

I don't tell you these stories to impress you or to imply that I'm some kind of saint. I'm certainly not. I've sinned many times in my life, including failures in this area of forgiveness. Nor am I an expert on the subject. I still have much to learn about the complicated work of forgiveness. However, over the past few decades I have gained some insights about the subject, both personally and professionally. What follows are some of the things I've learned.

The Costs of Unforgiveness

I'm writing this chapter during another flare-up in the Middle East between Israel and the Palestinians, this time in the Gaza Strip. The current conflict reminds me of a story that occurred several years ago in the Palestinian city of

Ramallah on the West Bank. Israel claimed that a terrorist from Ramallah attacked them. In response Israel's army came into Ramallah and wiped out huge sections of the city with tanks and bulldozers. During the assault, numerous Palestinians died. The next day the Palestinians, devastated by their losses, hung a huge banner on the town square of Ramallah. It said: "We will not forget. We will not forgive."

Of course, you don't have to go to the Middle East to see that kind of bitterness and lack of forgiveness. (That attitude can be found on *both* sides of the Israeli-Palestinian conflict.) You can see it lived out in any city, including your own. Tragically a lot of people live out those words: "I will not forget. I will not forgive." Their mother or father wounds them, and they say: "I will not forget. I will not forgive." Their spouse or ex-spouse hurts them, and they say: "I will not forget. I will not forgive." Their friend betrays them, and they say: "I will not forget. I will not forgive." Their coworker takes advantage of them, and they say: "I will not forget. I will not forgive." Their church disappoints them, and they say: "I will not forget. I will not forgive." And that bitterness, anger, and hostility become a cancer that eats them alive—emotionally, relationally, spiritually, and even physically.

Happiness expert Seligman writes that bitterness and lack of forgiveness "[block] the emotions of contentment and satisfaction and . . . makes serenity and peace impossible." He, along with other psychologists, argues that a person cannot experience life satisfaction while refusing to forgive. In short, a life of unforgiveness results in a life of unhappiness.[1]

A vivid illustration of this truth can be found in Mitch Albom's best-selling novel *The Five People You Meet in Heaven*. The main character in the book, a man named Eddie, died and went to heaven. But before he could fully enter heaven, he had to meet five people. These five people helped Eddie comes to terms with his life and make peace with himself and others. One of the five people Eddie met was a woman named Ruby. Ruby's job was to help Eddie come to terms with his father. Eddie's father abused him, both physically and verbally, leaving him deeply wounded. As a result Eddie responded with anger, bitterness, and hatred. Sadly Eddie's hatred of his father poisoned his soul. To be free he needed to forgive his dad. Ruby said to him, "Eddie, holding anger is poison. It eats you from inside. We think that hating is a weapon that attacks the person who harmed us. But hatred is a curved blade. And the harm we do, we do to ourselves."[2]

The Benefits of Forgiveness

We've seen some of the costs of not practicing forgiveness. The flip side of that coin is the massive benefit of practicing forgiveness. One leading expert in happiness research, Lyubomirsky, summarizes the benefits of forgiveness in the following quote: "Empirical research confirms this insight: Forgiving people are less likely to be hateful, depressed, hostile, anxious, angry, and neurotic. They are more likely to be happier, healthier, more agreeable, and more serene. They are better able to empathize with others and to be spiritual or religious. People who forgive hurts in relationships are more capable of reestablishing closeness. Finally, the inability to forgive is associated with persistent rumination or dwelling on revenge, while forgiving allows a person to move on."[3]

A biblical example of this important truth can be found in the story of Joseph in the book of Genesis. You may recall that Joseph's brothers deeply abused him, including throwing him down a well and then selling him into slavery. Eventually the slave traders sold him as a slave in a foreign land. Many years later Joseph made the decision to forgive his brothers. Genesis 45 records their reconciliation by saying, "Then he [Joseph] threw his arms around his brother Benjamin and wept, and Benjamin embraced him, weeping. And he kissed all his brothers and wept over them" (Gen. 45:14–15 NIV). Joseph's decision to forgive his brothers liberated both him and them from years of estrangement, reunited the entire family, and literally saved their lives.

A few years ago I preached a sermon at my church on the benefits of forgiveness. At the end of the sermon, we invited people to write down on a piece of paper a hurtful behavior against them that they needed and wanted to forgive. We then invited them to walk to the front of the church and place the pieces of paper into shredding machines, symbolizing their decision to forgive the infraction and let it go. Large numbers of people participated, including some who became emotionally overwhelmed by the experience. In the days and weeks afterward, I heard from several people who shared how powerfully that experience impacted them. One man told me that he had harbored bitterness against his ex-wife for many years and that it had poisoned his life in every possible way. But on that day, when he put a list of her infractions into the shredding machine at church, he chose to forgive her—and to forgive himself—for their failed relationship. He told me that it was the most life-giving and liberating decision of his entire adult life.

The Work of Forgiveness

Although forgiving others has massive benefits, it's still hard work. When I think about how difficult forgiveness can be, I'm reminded of the true story depicted in the movie *Dead Man Walking*. In that story a young man on drugs brutally rapes and murders a young woman. In time the murdered girl's father wants to forgive the murderer so that he can overcome his bitterness and find some peace. But how do you forgive someone who kills your daughter? The man, a Roman Catholic, decided to talk to a nun about it. He told her he wanted to forgive the man who killed his daughter, but he wasn't sure he ever could. He said to the nun, "I wish I had faith like you." His statement implied that if he had enough faith, he could forgive the murderer and move on with his life.

The nun wisely replied, "It's not that simple." Then she said, "It's not faith that allows us to forgive—it's work." She was absolutely right. Forgiveness is work—hard work. And it doesn't happen all of a sudden. It's a process. It takes time. For example, late in his life, the famous author C. S. Lewis said: "I think I have at last forgiven the cruel schoolmaster who so darkened my youth. I had done it many times before, but this time I think I have really done it." It took decades for C. S. Lewis to finally forgive this man. Forgiveness is hard work, and it takes time, but it's worth it.

Not long ago I read a book by Anne Lamott called *Plan B: Further Thoughts on Faith.* In this book Anne shares that her relationship with her mother was rocky, strained, and broken. When her mother died a few years ago, Anne had her body cremated. The funeral home placed her ashes in a brown box and gave them to Anne. Anne took her mother's ashes home, planning to place them on her bookshelf. But her anger toward her mother would not allow her to do it. Anne prayed, asking God to soften her heart and help her forgive her mom. But her heart remained hardened. So Anne put her mom's ashes in the back of her closet. She said, "I left her in the closet for two years to stew in her own ashes, and I refused to be nice to her, and I didn't forgive her for being a terrified, furious, clinging, sucking maw of need and arrogance."

Anne loved her mom, but she felt deep anger toward her. She said of her mom, "She was like someone who had broken my leg, and my leg had healed badly, and I would limp forever. . . . I couldn't, even after she died, grant her amnesty." So two years passed with her mom's ashes sitting in the back of the closet. Then one day she pulled out the ashes again. She discovered her heart did not feel as hard as it did two years earlier. But she still was not quite ready to forgive her mom, so Anne left the ashes in the closet for six more months. Then, on the anniversary of her mother's birthday, Anne once again took the box of ashes from her closet. She wrapped the box in birthday gift paper. Anne said, "I don't actually forgive her much yet . . . but I was not hating her anymore." So instead of putting the ashes back in the closet, she put them on a shelf in the living room. And that's where Anne ends the story. Although she had not yet fully forgiven her mom, Anne clearly was moving in that direction. I don't know for sure, but my guess is that Anne has, or will soon, finally forgive her mother. And when she does, the hard work of doing so will have been worth the effort.[4]

The Power of Forgiveness

Through the years I've seen, many times, the exceptional power of forgiveness. In fact, practicing forgiveness is the closest thing to a miracle I've ever witnessed. Forgiveness can transform people, institutions, and even nations, as we saw in postapartheid South Africa under Nelson Mandela. To help illustrate the power of forgiveness, I'd like to share with you the following true story.

At a United Methodist clergy meeting, I once met an African American minister named Fred. Way back in the 1970s, when race relations were especially strained, the bishop appointed Fred to pastor a large, all-white church. As you might guess, the appointment created quite a stir. A few weeks before moving to the church, Fred met with the district superintendent and the staff parish relations committee (personnel committee) of that church. On the committee served a lifelong member of the church, whose family had been members of that congregation for generations. This man totally and absolutely opposed Fred's appointment. He said to Fred, "No nigger is going to serve as pastor of this church." The district superintendent informed this racist man that the appointment was final and that he might as well accept it. The man looked directly at Fred and said, "I will do everything in my power to destroy your ministry here, even if I have to destroy this church in the process."

A few weeks later Fred showed up for his first Sunday at the church. Tensions were high. After the service this same man walked up to Fred and said the same words, "I will do everything in my power to destroy your ministry here, even if I have to destroy this church in the process." For the next few months, this man did everything he could to hurt Fred in both the church and the community. As you might expect, Fred began to hate this man almost as much as the man hated Fred. And then, unexpectedly, this man had a serious heart attack. Fred's first thought was, *God, let him die.*

This man had hurt Fred deeply, and Fred despised him. But regardless, Fred served as his pastor, so he went to the hospital. He met the man's wife in the intensive care waiting room and said: "Listen, I don't want to make things worse. If you don't think I should go in to see him, I won't."

The wife said, "I think you should go see him."

So Fred went into the intensive care room and saw this man, all hooked up to tubes and ventilators. Fred said, "I've come to let you know the people at church are praying for you, and so am I." Of course, Fred didn't tell him that he was praying God would let him die!

No response from the man. As Fred began to leave the room, the man reached out his hand. Fred hesitated. Finally he took the man's hand. The man squeezed Fred's hand, and something remarkable began to happen between the two of them. In the weeks ahead Fred visited this man on a regular basis. Both men felt a bit uneasy, but the tension decreased, and a tentative friendship began. A couple of months later, the man returned to church for the first time since his heart attack. It came time in the service for the sermon. As Fred walked to the pulpit to preach his sermon, this man walked to the front of the church. He said, "If you don't mind, Pastor, I'd like to say a few words." Fred felt uneasy about this unexpected interruption, but he let the man speak.

The man looked at the congregation and said, "All of you know that in recent months I've acted like a complete fool. I've come here today to tell you that I was dead wrong and to ask for your forgiveness." And then he turned to Fred and said, "And I've come here today to ask for your forgiveness as well."

At first Fred said nothing. This man had wounded him deep in his soul. But he knew the man spoke from the heart and that he needed to forgive him, and he actually wanted to forgive him. So Fred finally said, "I forgive you."

The man walked up to Fred, and, with tears in his eyes, he said to both Fred and the entire congregation, "I love my pastor." The man then embraced Fred, and Fred returned the embrace. Spontaneously, the congregation began to sing, "Blest be the tie that binds our hearts in Christian love." And although this was an all-white, uptight, United Methodist Church, one could hear a lot of "amens" and hand clapping, and some members even danced a bit in the pews.

Fred didn't preach his sermon that day; there was no need for one. That church had seen a sermon lived out, a sermon on the profound power of forgiveness. And that forgiveness transformed them. First, it transformed the man who had been so hateful to his pastor. After being forgiven by his church and his pastor, he experienced spiritual renewal in his life and was never the same again. Second, that forgiveness transformed the church. In the days ahead, God's spirit moved on that congregation in ways they had never experienced before. And finally, that forgiveness transformed Fred. By forgiving a racist white man who had hurt him deeply, Fred released some of his own racism, anger, and bitterness and found a peace he had never known before. Such is the liberating and transforming power of forgiveness. That's why Jesus taught us to pray, "Forgive us our sins as we forgive those who sin against us."

The Gift of Forgiveness

As you probably know, forgiveness is a major biblical theme and a huge emphasis of Jesus. As I've studied what the Bible teaches about forgiveness, I've concluded that at heart, forgiveness is a gift, in at least three ways.

First, forgiveness is a *gift to others*. As Colossians says, "Bear with one another and, if anyone has a complaint against another, forgive each other; just as the Lord has forgiven you, so you also must forgive" (3:13). When we obey this command to forgive others—including our spouse, children, parents, friends, coworkers, and fellow church members—we give them a great gift.

Second, forgiveness is a *gift to God*. In the Gospel of Luke, Jesus said, "But love your enemies, do good to them . . . and you will be children of the Most High, because he is kind to the ungrateful and wicked. Be merciful, just as your Father is merciful" (6:35–36 NIV). One of the main reasons we are called to forgive others is because we are children of God. Since God forgives, God wants God's children to forgive.

So forgiveness is not only a gift to others; it's also a gift to God, and it brings God joy.

Finally, forgiveness is a *gift to ourselves*. Jesus once said, "Forgive others, and you will be forgiven. Give, and you will receive. Your gift will return to you in full—pressed down, shaken together to make room for more, running over, and poured into your lap. The amount you give will determine the amount you get back" (Luke 6:37–38 NLT). When we forgive others, not only do we give a gift to others and to God, but we also give a gift to ourselves. Research shows that when we forgive others, it benefits us relationally, emotionally, spiritually, and even physically. When we let go of the anger and bitterness we harbor toward people who have wronged us, it's absolutely liberating. I once heard an unusual story about a man who wore a heavy winter coast on blistering hot summer days. When asked why he wore it, he replied, "Because it feels so good when I take it off." When we take off our resentment against others and forgive them, it feels good. In short, forgiving others is one of the best gifts we can ever give to ourselves.

The Process of Forgiveness

Before concluding, we need to talk about how to forgive. Unfortunately, no simple, clear-cut formula exists for successfully forgiving people. Forgiveness is hard, takes time, and is often messy. For example, we might forgive someone and feel our work is done. However, later on, we once again feel our old resentment returning toward them, and we have to start all over again. As Lyubomirsky says, "Forgiveness is a strategy that takes a great deal of effort, willpower, and motivation. It must be practiced."[5]

However, we can take steps that will help us forgive. For example, when I'm trying to forgive someone, I pray for them. It's hard to resent someone whom you pray for on a regular basis. In my prayers for that person, I also ask God to help me forgive them. Another strategy I've found helpful is writing a letter of forgiveness. In that letter I fully express how that person hurt me. But I also clearly communicate that I choose to forgive them. I rarely send those letters because they can seriously backfire. But writing such letters has helped me on numerous occasions. Another step we can take is to talk to a friend, a pastor, or even a counselor about our efforts to forgive. Having a friend to help us on the journey of forgiveness is exceptionally productive. Another helpful step is to remember that God has forgiven us for all our sins and, in return, asks us to forgive others. That doesn't make it easy. However, it does give us a powerful, spiritual motivation to practice forgiveness.

Seligman offers a five-step process called "REACH" for forgiving people. This process of forgiveness comes from a psychologist named Everett Worthington. In this acrostic *R* stands for "recall." Forgiveness begins by objectively recalling the hurt you have experienced. The *E* stands for "empathize." In this step you attempt to understand the person who hurt you from his or her perspective. The *A* stands for "altruistic." In this step you attempt to rise above your anger and desire for vengeance and choose to be altruistic and forgiving. The *C* stands for "commit." In this step you commit yourself to forgiving the person, even writing down a "certificate of forgiveness." The *H* stands for "hold." In this difficult step you continue to hold on to your forgiveness of the person, even when memories of the painful event recur. Although Seligman admits that these five steps of forgiveness may sound "mushy and preachy," he argues that they are based on solid research, they work, and, in the end, they are worth the effort.[6] Jesus would agree.

Forgiveness Principles

In one of my previous books, I listed several forgiveness principles. I think it would be beneficial to repeat those principles before concluding this chapter:

1. *Forgiveness is hard work.* Forgiving other people is a challenge, especially when the infraction is major. Forgiving someone is not easy. It's not natural. It takes discipline and effort. It's worth the effort, but it's not easy.
2. *Forgiveness can take time.* Minor infractions, like the inevitable day-to-day conflicts in marriage and family life, can often be forgiven immediately, without significant effort. But for major infractions, forgiveness can take years. It's a process. It takes time to let go of our hurt and fully forgive.
3. *Forgiveness does not mean we condone bad behavior.* You can fully forgive someone but not accept or condone the behavior. This is especially true in cases of crime or abuse. For example, you can forgive someone for abusing you, but you absolutely do not condone the behavior.
4. *Forgiveness does not always result in reconciliation.* It's beautiful when it does, but that is not always the case. The person we forgive may not acknowledge a need for forgiveness. The person we forgive might be dead. The person we forgive might be dangerous—mentally unstable or even a criminal—and should not be contacted. Forgiving someone does not always repair the relationship.
5. *Forgiveness is primarily for our benefit.* Harboring bitterness and resentment and anger toward another person deeply damages us—emotionally, spiritually, and even physically. In order to be liberated from bitterness, we must choose to forgive the person who hurt us and move forward with our life. Ultimately, forgiveness helps us more than it helps the person who is forgiven.[7]

I Remember Forgetting That

I once heard a story about a woman named Clara. Throughout her life, Clara tried to live out God's command to forgive others. Like many Christians, Clara prayed the Lord's Prayer every day, including the words, "Forgive us our trespasses as we forgive those who trespass against us." Clara not only prayed these words; she practiced them. One day Clara ate lunch with an old friend. The friend recalled a cruel thing someone had done to Clara a few years earlier. Clara seemed not to remember. Her friend could not believe it because the infraction was horrible. Clara's friend said, "Don't you remember that awful thing Mary Jane did to you?"

"No," said Clara, "I distinctly remember forgetting that."

CHAPTER 6

CONTENTED PEOPLE
PRACTICE GENEROSITY

A generous person will be enriched, and one who gives water will get water.

—Proverbs 11:25

The Dalai Lama once said, "If you want *others* to be happy, practice compassion. If *you* want to be happy, practice compassion." Science, Scripture, and experience all agree with the Dalai Lama. If you and I want to give and receive happiness, we must engage in the practice of generosity.

Generosity and Science

The science is unambiguous. Practicing generosity creates happiness, as the following quotes from three leading happiness experts confirm:

- "Being generous and willing to share makes people happy." —Sonja Lyubomirsky, *The How of Happiness*[1]
- "We scientists have found that doing a kindness produces the single most reliable momentary increase in well-being of any exercise we have tested." —Martin Seligman, *Flourish*[2]
- "People who care about other people are on average happier than those who are more preoccupied with themselves." —Richard Layard, *Happiness*[3]

Research on the connection between generosity and happiness is overwhelming. For example, a few years ago the National Institute of Neurological Disorders in Bethesda, Maryland, conducted a fascinating research project. They gave a significant sum of money to volunteers and then studied their brain waves. After receiving the money, the volunteers had to make a choice. They could keep the money for themselves, or they could give it away to charity. They made their decision while hooked up to a brain machine called functional magnetic resonance imaging (MRI), which maps activity in the brain. The scientists discovered that when people give their money away to charity, it impacts the brain's reward center, the part of the brain that causes feelings of joy and euphoria. The researchers concluded that acts of financial generosity make a physiological impact on people, resulting in feelings of happiness, well-being, and contentment. And the impact wasn't just short term. The researchers also learned that when people are generous, hormones are released that have a long-term impact on happiness. In short, science has discovered that generosity leads to happiness.[4]

Generosity and Scripture

The Bible also teaches that generosity leads to contentment and well-being, as we see in the following passages.

- "Some give freely, yet grow all the richer; others withhold what is due, and only suffer want. A generous person will be enriched, and one who gives water will get water." (Prov. 11:24–25)
- "He [Jesus] himself said, 'It is more blessed to give than to receive.'" (Acts 20:35)
- "He sat down, called the twelve, and said to them, 'Whoever wants to be first must be last of all and servant of all.'" (Mark 9:35)

Scripture is clear. When we practice generosity, we receive a blessing. Giving of our time, money, kindness, encouragement, love, and service enriches us. When we practice generosity, it makes us bigger, more complete, and more fulfilled. As Proverbs says, "Happy are those who are kind to the poor" (14:21). Therefore, throughout the Bible, God consistently encourages us to practice generosity. For example, 1 Timothy says, "Be generous and willing to share" (6:18 NIV).

A powerful example of how generosity toward others brings life satisfaction can be found in Isaiah 58. In this passage the prophet Isaiah says that when we fight for justice, feed the hungry, shelter the homeless, and clothe the naked, we experience renewal, healing, and the presence of God. Isaiah goes on to say that when we serve others, we dispel the darkness in our lives and live in the light. Finally, Isaiah affirms that when we extend generosity, we flourish "like a watered garden, like a spring of water, whose waters never fail" (58:11). Of course, as Christian believers, our primary purpose for practicing generosity is not to be blessed but to be faithful to God. Thankfully, a side benefit of doing so is increased contentment.

Generosity and Experience

Experience confirms what scientific research has discovered and Scripture teaches. If I've learned anything in three decades of ministry, it's that generous people are happy people. I see that truth virtually every day of my life. The most miserable folks I know are not people who suffer serious illness or experience significant loss. Instead, the saddest people I know are stingy, self-absorbed people who spend all their time, money, and energy on themselves. Stingy people have small hearts and souls and never find true joy and contentment in their lives, even if they have a lot of money. Why? Because self is too small a god to serve. If our life is only about us, we will never experience fulfillment. In short, a self-absorbed life offers a ticket to a miserable life.

On the other hand, the happiest folks I know are people who practice generosity with their time, kindness, encouragement, money, and service. When people share what they have with others, they experience joy, contentment, and happiness. If you and I want to be happy, we need to practice generosity. To further illustrate this truth, I'd like to tell you two stories, one from my professional experience and one from my personal experience.

"This Is My Room!"

A couple of years ago my church raised funds for and then built a Habitat for Humanity house. Hundreds of people participated by generously giving their money, their time, or both. After completing the project, we held a dedication service at the site. After the dedication service people went inside to look at the house. The family receiving the house had four children. The youngest child, a little girl about seven years old, grabbed my hand and walked me and another person to her room. She never had a room of her own before; she always shared one with her siblings. With great excitement she began to run around the room in circles. Shouting at the top of her lungs, she screamed, "This is my room! This is my room!" Her unbridled joy brought tears to my eyes and happiness to my heart. I can't remember a time that I felt more satisfied or content in my pastoral work. When I shared that story with my congregation the next Sunday, tears flowed, and a spirit of happiness overpowered the room.

Finding Joy at Walgreens

I once stood in line at a Walgreens pharmacy, waiting to pick up some routine prescriptions. The woman in front of me had three children in tow and appeared frazzled. One of her children looked seriously ill. She told the pharmacy clerk that she needed to pick up several prescriptions for her child. When the clerk rang up the charges, the woman looked mortified. As she fumbled through her wallet, she became embarrassed. Finally she said, "I don't have enough money to pay for these." So she paid for the least expensive medication and told the clerk she would try to return later for the other two. As she walked away, I noticed tears in her eyes.

Although I did not know her, I felt compassion for this woman who could not afford to buy medicine for her sick child. Although I've never struggled to afford health care for my children, I knew at that moment that it must feel devastating. After purchasing my prescriptions, I said to the clerk, "I'd like to pay for that woman's medicine." The clerk looked confused, so I repeated my request. After a moment of hesitation, she went to get the manager. I explained to the manager what just happened. Then I told him I'd like to pay for the woman's medicine but that I wanted to do it anonymously. He agreed to the request. They promised to call the woman that afternoon and inform her that her child's medicine had been paid for by an anonymous donor. Later that afternoon the pharmacy called me and said they successfully reached her, that she returned for the meds, and that she expressed overwhelming joy and gratitude for the gift. In fact, they said she just about danced in the store! The money I spent did not represent a major sacrifice for me. But that spontaneous "random act of kindness" brought me enormous happiness. Even now, as I write these words, the memory brings joy to my heart. Jesus certainly knew what he was talking about when he said, "It is more blessed to give than to receive."

A Little Pail of Tears

While working on my doctorate, I studied theology under a professor named Vernon Davis. One day during class Dr. Davis told us a story from his first pastorate after seminary. During his first week on the job, he went to visit the matriarch of the congregation. A charter member in her nineties, she knew everything about the church. They had a pleasant visit, and Dr. Davis learned many interesting things about his new congregation. As he left, the woman said something that Dr. Davis claims was "the best pastoral advice I ever received." The elderly woman said, "Reverend Davis, when you come to church on Sunday morning, we'll all be wearing nice clothes, and we'll all smile at you. And when you ask us how we are doing, we'll all say we are doing fine. But don't let that fool you. Just remember that under every heart is a little pail of tears."

All people on earth carry a little pail of tears under our hearts. We've all been wounded in some way. All of us carry at least some pain in our hearts and souls. One of the great benefits of generosity is that it can help heal our wounds.

The Healing Power of Generosity

You may have heard of Karl Menninger, a famous psychiatrist, now deceased. He once gave a speech on mental health and then opened it up for questions. A man asked him, "What would you advise a person to do if he or she felt a nervous breakdown coming on?" Most people in the crowd expected Menninger to say, "Consult a psychiatrist." To their astonishment he replied, "If a person feels a nervous breakdown coming, they should lock up their house, go across the railway track, find someone in need, and do something to help that person."

Karl Menninger understood that when we help heal other people, we find healing for ourselves. That's what Jesus meant when he said, "Those who lose their life . . . will find it" (Matt. 10:39). As Saint Francis of Assisi said in his famous prayer, "For it is in giving that we receive." When we help other people find healing, a part of us is also healed.

That proved true for a former U.S. Marine named Tim. Tim lost one of his legs during combat in Iraq. One day, while cleaning his attic, he came across a couple of his old artificial legs. He figured that someone could probably use them, especially since they are so expensive. But he didn't know where he could donate them. After several failed attempts to find a donation site, he took matters into his own hands. Tim began an organization called "Operation Arise and Walk," a collection point for used artificial limbs. He houses the nonprofit organization in his garage, where he collects, repairs, and ships the artificial limbs to land-mine victims around the world. With the help of numerous volunteers, Tim has shipped hundreds of artificial legs and feet to help amputees in Central America. Tim knows the feelings of hopelessness and suffering caused by losing a limb. He once said, "By helping others, I'm putting myself back together." When we practice generosity by giving of our time, money, and service to help others, we experience healing ourselves, as the following story teaches.

The Magical Mustard Seed

In this ancient legend a woman's only son died. In her grief she went to a holy man and said, "What magical incantations do you have to heal my grief?"

He said to her: "Fetch me a mustard seed from a home that has never known sorrow. We will use it to drive the sorrow out of your life."

The woman went off at once in search of that magical mustard seed. She came first to a splendid mansion, knocked at the door, and said: "I am looking for a home that has never known sorrow. Is this such a place?"

They told her, "You've certainly come to the wrong place," and they began to describe all the tragic things that had recently befallen them.

The woman said to herself, "Who better able to help these poor, unfortunate people than me, having had misfortune of my own?" So she stayed to comfort them and then went on in search of a home that had never known sorrow. But wherever she turned, in hovels and in mansions, she found one tale after another of sadness and misfortune. She became so involved in ministering to other people's grief that ultimately she forgot about her quest for the magical mustard seed, never realizing that it had, in fact, driven the sorrow out of her life.

Finding Ways to Serve

Literally hundreds of options exist for practicing generosity, from random acts of kindness to organized service projects, both short and long term. Perhaps the best way to practice generosity is to do so with your time and your money. Countless opportunities exist for doing so, both in your church and in your community. For example, people in my congregation give significant amounts of money every year. A large percentage of those funds go directly to ministries that help people, both locally and beyond. Large numbers of our congregation also volunteer their time to serve others in various capacities, including our food pantry that provides groceries to about eight hundred people every week. Your church and community provide similar opportunities to practice generosity. All you have to do is look.

Unfortunately, Americans are not as generous as we could be, including financially. For example, average American Christians give less than 2 percent of their income to charity, and that includes both religious and secular causes. That's a far cry from the biblical standard of a tithe (10 percent of our income). We live in the most affluent country in the world. Given that reality, we need to seriously consider Jesus' words, "To whom much has been given, much will be required" (Luke 12:48). The same dynamic is true of service. While many Americans regularly engage in service to others, large numbers do not. However, as we've already seen, science, Scripture, and experience tell us that if we want to experience true contentment, we need to practice generosity with both our time and our money. I'd like to close this chapter by telling you about a congregation that learned firsthand that generosity leads to happiness.

Christmas at First Church

Several years ago a United Methodist church in North Carolina learned about the joy of service, both individually and as a congregation. This church, concerned about homeless people in their town, especially during the winter months, spearheaded a program to help. They, along with fourteen other churches in their city, committed to care for homeless people for one week each winter. Each church opened up its facilities, usually the fellowship hall, to care for eighteen to twenty homeless guests. They provided a warm and safe place to sleep, along with meals and other assistance throughout the week.

In early November the cooperating churches gathered for their final organizational meeting. The agenda included scheduling a specific week for each church during the winter months. The United Methodist pastor planned to go to the meeting. However, given her busy schedule, she asked a woman from her church to go in her place. This woman, a new Christian and new church member, was an enthusiastic and devoted layperson. The pastor gave her a list of convenient weeks in January and February for their congregation to care for the homeless group. The pastor told her, "Make sure to schedule us for one of these weeks."

The woman went to the meeting. But not long into the meeting, they reached an impasse. Not one of the fifteen cooperating churches expressed willingness to take Christmas week. First, it interfered with all their Christmas activities, including Christmas Eve services. Second, everybody knew their members would not want to cook meals and provide other services for homeless folks during the Christmas holidays. This woman, an enthusiastic new Christian believer, felt dumbfounded. She could not believe that none of the churches would take the week of Christmas. In fact, the more they argued about who was going to have to take Christmas, the madder this woman got. Before she knew it, she smashed her hand down on the table, stood up, and gave a speech. "I can't believe this," she exclaimed. "Jesus and his family were homeless in Bethlehem on the very first Christmas, and yet not one church in this community is willing to care for homeless people during the week of Christmas. Shame on you!"

The pastors all felt ashamed but not ashamed enough to volunteer for the week of Christmas! When nobody volunteered, this laywoman boldly proclaimed, "My church, the First United Methodist Church, will take Christmas week, not only this year but every year." One of the pastors said, "So moved." Another said, "I'll second that." After a quick vote, the meeting adjourned.

After leaving the meeting, this woman went to see her pastor, full of excitement. She said: "I have great news! Our church gets to care for homeless people during the week of Christmas not only this year but every year! Isn't that great?" Well, that wasn't exactly great news to the pastor. What about their Christmas Eve services? How would they find volunteers to cook and care for homeless people during the holidays? No, this was not good news at all to the pastor. She deeply regretted not going to the meeting herself. But what could she do? It was a done deal.

The next Sunday the pastor gave the news to her congregation. She said, "We are going to host homeless people during the week of Christmas, and we need a bunch of volunteers to help." She didn't think she would get any response, but her assumption proved wrong. People came out of the woodwork to volunteer. Families with young children volunteered, saying to the pastor, "We want our kids to know there is more to Christmas than getting presents." Families who had lost loved ones during the year volunteered, hoping to fill the void of the Christmas season.

The pastor almost received more volunteers than she could use. Christmas week finally arrived. Eighteen homeless people came to the Methodist church to spend the week. And much to this pastor's surprise, it ended up being the highlight of the year for the church.

People brought in loads of food. The homeless guests ate like kings all week. Church members also brought nice clothes and coats for them to wear. They brought gifts for everyone, especially the children. And they didn't just give food, clothes, and gifts—they gave of themselves as well. People stayed for hours to visit with the group. They ate meals with them and played games with them. They even held a marathon, three-day-long Monopoly tournament! Many members spent one or more nights during the week. The church members got to know these people as *real* people. Although they were not required to go, all eighteen of the homeless guests went to the Christmas Eve Candlelight Communion service. The congregation warmly welcomed them, and everyone in attendance had a holy moment. In fact, the entire week ended up being a glorious experience for the church, and it continued that way for the next five years.

This story has an unusual ending. After six years of hosting homeless folks during the week of Christmas, the Methodist pastor received a phone call from the Baptist pastor. He said: "Everyone in town has heard how much your church enjoys hosting the homeless group at Christmas. So we wondered if you would you be willing to share that week with some of the other churches? We were hoping we could do Christmas week this year."

This United Methodist church in North Carolina learned something profound through this experience. They learned that true contentment comes not by taking care of our own needs but by taking care of others' needs. Jesus was right. It is more blessed to give than to receive.

CHAPTER 7

CONTENTED PEOPLE
NURTURE RELATIONSHIPS

Two are better than one, because they have a good return for their labor: If either of them falls down, one can help the other up.
— Ecclesiastes 4:9–10 NIV

The ancient Greek philosopher Epicurus once said that of all the things that contribute to happiness, "the greatest by far is the possession of friendship." Although Epicurus lived hundreds of years before the time of Christ, he clearly understood that life satisfaction heavily depends on nurturing significant relationships.

A few months ago I went on a retreat. During one of the sessions, our presenter asked each participant to write down on paper a brief statement of our self-identity. I wrote:

"I am a . . .

- husband,
- father,
- grandfather,
- friend,

- pastor,
- author, and
- beloved child of God."

When I reviewed my statement the next day, I realized that those seven identities encapsulated the core essence of my being. I also noticed that six of the seven identities (all but author) are highly relational, and those relationships bring great joy and contentment to my life. It reminded me once again that relationships—with God and others—are the bottom line of a good life, as Jesus taught us in the Great Commandment when he told us to love God and neighbor.

Most people realize that life satisfaction heavily depends on nurturing significant relationships. This, probably more than any other factor, leads to a contented life, which reminds me of a cheesy story that I still enjoy telling.

The Big Rocks

A well-known time-management guru once gave a speech at a top-drawer business school. As he stood in front of a class of high-powered overachievers, he said, "OK, it's time for a quiz." He pulled out a one-gallon, wide-mouthed Mason jar and set it on the table in front of him. He then produced about a dozen fist-sized rocks and carefully placed them in the jar. After filling the jar to the top, he asked, "Is this jar full?" Everyone in the class said yes.

"Really?" he asked. He then reached under the table and pulled out a bucket of gravel. He poured the gravel into the jar, shaking it as he did, causing pieces of gravel to work themselves into the spaces between the big rocks. Then he asked the group once more, "Is the jar full?" By now the class was on to him.

"Probably not," one of them answered.

"Good answer!" he replied. He reached under the table and brought out a bucket of sand. He dumped the sand into the jar, filling all the spaces between the rocks and the gravel. Once more he asked the question, "Is this jar full?"

"No!" the class shouted.

Once again he said, "Good answer!" Then he took a pitcher of water and poured it until the jar was filled to the brim. He looked at the class and asked, "What is the point of this illustration?"

One eager student said, "No matter how full your schedule, if you try really hard, you can always fit more into it."

"No," the speaker replied, "that's not the point. The point is—if you don't put the big rocks in first, you'll never get them in at all."

So what are the big rocks? Of all the things that clamor for our time, energy, and attention, what matters most? The answer from Scripture, science, and experience is clear. Relationships with others are the big rocks.

Relationship Research

Positive psychology research has overwhelmingly concluded that nurturing relationships with others is a primary key in attaining happiness and life satisfaction. A few brief examples follow.

- "The pursuit of relationships is a rock-bottom fundamental to human well-being." —Martin Seligman, *Flourish*[1]
- "People who are in loving relationships with another adult have better hormonal balance and better health, and are of course happier." —Richard Layard, *Happiness*[2]
- "One conclusion was blatantly clear from my happiness research: everyone from contemporary scientists to ancient philosophers agrees that having strong social

bonds is probably the *most* meaningful contributor to happiness." —Gretchen Rubin, *The Happiness Project*[3]

- "Very happy people differed markedly from average people and from unhappy people in one principal way: a rich and fulfilling social life." —Martin Seligman, *Authentic Happiness*[4]
- "Relationships constitute the single most important factor [in living a happy life]. . . . Investing in social relationships is a potent strategy on the path to becoming happier." —Sonja Lyubomirsky, *The How of Happiness*[5]

The science is clear and unambiguous. Healthy relationships are at the center of a well-lived and contented life. On this important topic, science and Scripture once again concur. To illustrate, we'll review both an Old Testament and a New Testament example.

"Two Are Better than One"

As noted in chapter 1, the writer of the book of Ecclesiastes spent his entire adult life seeking meaning and happiness. In chapter 4, the Teacher of Ecclesiastes affirms that nurturing relationships is a major key in attaining contentment. However, in keeping with his overall pessimistic and cynical tone, Ecclesiastes begins on a negative note before the writer moves to a positive one, as we can see in the following verses: "Again, I saw vanity under the sun: the case of solitary individuals, without sons or brothers; yet there is no end to all their toil, and their eyes are never satisfied with riches. 'For whom am I toiling,' they ask, 'and depriving myself of pleasure?' This also is vanity and an unhappy business" (4:7–8).

What a sad passage. Ecclesiastes speaks about people who work hard and make good money but have no meaningful relationships. They are, in Ecclesiastes' words, "solitary individuals." This text reminds me of an old Beatles song, recently made into a trilogy of movies called *The Disappearance of Eleanor Rigby*. The haunting refrain of the song "Eleanor Rigby" asks, "All the lonely people, where do they all come from?"

Loneliness is a huge problem in America and has been for a long time. Way back in 1970, Philip Slater wrote a groundbreaking and classic book on the subject called *The Pursuit of Loneliness*. Since then, the problem has only grown worse. Numerous people have explored why so many Americans feel so lonely. One such person is therapist and author Will Miller. In his book, *Refrigerator Rights*, Miller convincingly argues that the American way of life erodes meaningful relationships. According to Miller, many factors contribute to American feelings of isolation, including the following:

- Americans frequently move.
- Americans overvalue independence.
- Americans are driven to succeed.
- Americans are overwhelmingly busy.
- Americans are consumed with materialism.
- Americans are diverted by media.
- Americans expect too much from their spouse.[6]

Other reasons for our growing loneliness and isolation as a nation could be noted. But clearly many people in America do not experience contentment because they lack social connections. According to our text in Ecclesiastes, this relationship void among "solitary individuals" is "unhappy business." Ecclesiastes notes that hard work and financial success are no substitute for being connected to other human beings. Although he comes at it from a negative point of view, the Teacher of Ecclesiastes clearly communicates: "What matters most in life is being connected with other persons. We are not meant to live in isolation from others. God did not intend for us to be loners in this life." In short, Ecclesiastes confirms that one of the primary keys to contentment is developing a network of strong relationships. Although he says that negatively in verses 4:7–8, he says it positively in the verses that follow: "Two are better than one, because they have a good reward for their toil. For if they fall, one will lift up the other; but woe to one who is alone and falls and does not have another to help. Again, if two lie together, they keep warm; but how can one keep warm alone? And though one might prevail against another, two will withstand one. A threefold cord is not quickly broken" (4:9–12).

Although we often hear the words "two are better than one" at weddings, Ecclesiastes is not taking about marriage. Instead, he's referring to relationships in general. In this text Ecclesiastes affirms that if we want a good life, we must live it in connection with other people. After highlighting the value of being connected to others, he notes several specific benefits of close relationships. First, relationships give us support when we fall (v. 10). Second, relationships give us warmth (v. 11). And third, relationships give us strength for facing life's battles (v. 12).

Ecclesiastes' comments about the need for friendships reminds me of a story about a woman named Janice. When her doctor told her that she had cancer and needed a radical mastectomy, she felt devastated. She said: "It was impossible to comprehend what was about to happen. I cried hysterically. I could not imagine what it would be like. It was so inconceivable that I was actually living this nightmare." A week before her surgery, she almost decided to cancel the surgery, give up, and die. Only one thing kept her from doing so. That evening she thumbed through the day's mail. She noticed a postcard from a close friend. Her friend wrote just one word on the postcard, scrawled in big letters. The one word was "LIVE!" Janice taped the postcard on her bathroom mirror and left it there through her surgery, chemo, radiation, and all the follow-up visits. She later said, "Whenever I felt tempted to give up, I would look at that word and repeat it again and again and again. Live! Live! Live!" And you know what? She did.

The message of Ecclesiastes 4:7–12 is clear. If we want to have a contented life, we must invest ourselves into relationships, in spite of all their messiness, hard work, and potential for pain because "two are better than one."

What Would Jesus Do?

Like the writer of Ecclesiastes, Jesus knew that "two are better than one." In spite of his God-given mission and highly demanding schedule, Jesus made relationships with others a major priority in his life. We see this in at least two ways.

First, *Jesus nurtured individual relationships*. For example, Jesus enjoyed a close friendship with Lazarus and his sisters, Mary and Martha. In John we read, "Jesus loved Martha and her sister and Lazarus" (11:5). Lazarus, Mary, and Martha were dear friends of Jesus. He often went to visit them at their home in Bethany. In fact, during the last few days of his life, when everything was falling apart, Jesus went to Bethany to see them. He needed their love and support in good times and especially in hard times. In the biblical story of Lazarus's death, Jesus walked to his grave. When he arrived, the Bible says, "Jesus began to weep. So the Jews said, 'See how he loved him!'" (John 11:35–36). Clearly Jesus deeply loved Lazarus, Mary, and Martha. He invested significant time and energy into his friendship with them.

Second, *Jesus nurtured group relationships*. In Mark 3 we read, "He appointed twelve, whom he also named apostles, to be with him" (v. 14). Jesus knew he could not do his work alone. So he gathered a small group of twelve disciples to join him. They worked together, prayed together, laughed together, cried together, and sometimes fought together. These twelve men became Jesus' dear friends. We clearly see that in Mark 14. By this point in his ministry, Jesus found himself in deep trouble with both religious and political authorities. The cross loomed. Jesus knew his life was almost over. So he turned to his group of friends for support. The text says, "They went to a place called Gethsemane, and Jesus said to his disciples, 'Sit here while I pray.' He took Peter, James, and John along with him, and he began to be deeply distressed and troubled. 'My soul is overwhelmed with sorrow to the point of death,' he said to them. 'Stay here and keep watch'" (Mark 14:32–34 NIV). Even Jesus "the Christ, the Son of the living God" (Matt. 16:16 KJV) was not self-sufficient. Like us Jesus needed and wanted comrades for the journey. So he immersed himself into a small group of twelve friends.

Fossils and Friendship

I once watched a fascinating television show on the History Channel. It told about a group of paleontologists who found the fossil remains of an ancient human being. When they examined the fossilized bones, they discovered the man's leg had been badly broken but then healed. They came to the conclusion that this person must have had a community to care for him. Had he been a "solitary individual," in the words of Ecclesiastes, he would have died right away. The elements and wild animals would have killed him within days. But this man was part of a community who cared for him until his leg healed and he could fend for himself again.

The truth is that every person is broken in some way. If we're not broken physically, then we're broken emotionally, spiritually, or relationally. And the only way broken people can survive is by having others help us with our wounds. Like the ancient man with the broken leg, we all need others to support us. That kind of supportive friendship is one of the primary tasks of the church. Christianity is not an individual religion but a community religion. As I noted in my previous book, Christianity is a "we" religion, not a "me" religion.⁷ God has called the church to love and support and encourage one another. On a practical level that mostly plays out in small groups within a congregation. So if you want Christian friends to support you in good times and in bad times, then you, like Jesus, need to connect with a small group.

I learned a long time ago that I am not self-sufficient. Instead, I desperately need relationships in my life. So I try to follow Jesus' example and work hard at maintaining several individual relationships. That obviously includes my wife, children, granddaughter, and other family members. But it also includes friends beyond my family. Like Jesus, I try to maintain several "Lazarus" friendships. Those special friendships are more important to me than almost anything.

Not only do I maintain individual friendships, but I also have a group of friends. For example, I belong to a clergy support group. We gather together regularly to support one another, to laugh together and sometimes cry together, and to bat ideas off one another. It takes commitment and effort to keep that group alive. But I couldn't make it without them. Like the writer of Ecclesiastes and Jesus, I have learned that "two are better than one."

The Bottom Line

It's beyond the scope of this book to serve as a relationship manual. However, it needs to be noted that maintaining good relationships with family, friends, neighbors, coworkers, and fellow church members is hard work. Prioritizing the relationships in our life takes a lot of time and energy. Relationships require enormous effort to maintain, including a lot of grace and forgiveness because all of us are imperfect people. And relationships are often messy and sometimes bring great pain to our lives. But in the end, other than our faith in God, relationships with others are what matter most. When we get to the end of our life, it's not going to matter what our net worth is, or how many diplomas hang on the wall, or how many career awards we won. When we get to the end of our life, what's going to matter is our relationships with the people we love.

On 9/11, when people in the World Trade Center began to realize that they would not get out alive, they made a lot of phone calls and left a lot of messages. However, they didn't call their bosses to tell them about unfinished work projects. They didn't call their financial advisers to make stock transactions. Instead, they called the people in their lives, both family and friends, and said, "I love you."

The bottom line is that relationships are primary. They are the big rocks. Two are indeed better than one. Because of that, the relationships in our lives are worth all the effort it takes to maintain them and even the pain they sometimes bring. Therefore, if we want to live a life of contentment, we must constantly nurture our relationships with others.

Someone's Hand to Hold

I once heard a story about a rabbi who went to the beach for vacation. As he sat on the beach, he watched two children playing in the sand. They worked hard building an elaborate sand castle by the water's edge, with gates, towers, and even a moat. They had almost completed their sand castle when a big wave came along and knocked it down, reducing it to a heap of wet sand. The rabbi expected the children to burst into tears, devastated by the loss of all their hard work. But the children surprised him. Instead of crying, they held each other's hand, laughed a big belly laugh, and sat down to build another castle. The rabbi said he learned an important lesson from those children that day. All the things in our lives, all the complicated structures we spent so much time and energy creating, are built on sand. Sooner or later a wave will come along and knock down what we have worked so hard to build up. And when that happens, only the person who has somebody's hand to hold will be able to laugh and rebuild.

CHAPTER 8

CONTENTED PEOPLE
EXPRESS GRATITUDE

Give thanks in all circumstances; for this is God's will for you.
—1 Thessalonians 5:18 NIV

Before her recent retirement, Barbara Walters interviewed the well-known comedian Ellen DeGeneres. During the interview Ellen told some of her life story. Like many entertainers she faced some tough times, especially early in her career. However, at the time of the interview, things were going exceptionally well for Ellen, in both her personal and her professional life, for which she expressed deep gratitude. During the interview, Ellen talked about her first big break in the entertainment business. Years ago she appeared on *The Tonight Show* and performed a comedy routine where she called God on the telephone. It proved hugely successful and helped launch her career to a new level. Near the end of the interview, Barbara Walters referred to Ellen's comedy routine about talking to God on the telephone. Barbara asked Ellen, "If you could talk to God on the phone today, what would you say?" Without a moment's hesitation Ellen said, "I'd say thank you."

Throughout this book we are exploring what science and Scripture teach about contentment. Once again both disciplines converge when it comes to gratitude. Every major positive psychologist in the country agrees that grateful people are happier people. For example, Seligman says, "Gratitude can make your life happier and more satisfying."[1] Lyubomirsky says, "The expression of gratitude is a kind of metastrategy for achieving happiness."[2] Scripture teaches the same thing. Expressing thanksgiving is a major theme throughout the Bible. For example, Psalm 95:2 says, "Let us come before him with thanksgiving" (NIV). First Thessalonians 5:18 says, "Give thanks in all circumstances; for this is the will of God in Christ Jesus for you." My own experience, both personally and professionally, affirms the same conclusion as science and Scripture. I've seen firsthand the life-giving benefits of gratitude. I've also seen the life-diminishing results of not practicing gratitude. Clearly expressing gratitude is a crucial key to experiencing life satisfaction and contentment.

The Enemy of Gratitude

Before further exploring the benefits of gratitude, let's first review the biggest obstacle to practicing it—envy and the resentment that follows. To make the point, we'll turn to an old Jewish legend about a poor farmer who constantly struggled to survive. Then one night everything changed. According to the legend, an angel of God came to him and said: "You have found favor in the eyes of God. As a result God wants to bless you. Therefore, make three requests, and God will grant them. There's only one condition—your neighbor will get a double portion of everything God gives to you."

The next morning the farmer told his wife about the three wishes. She suggested they put the dream to a test. So they decided on their first wish. The poor farmer prayed, "O God, I would like to have a thousand head of cattle, which would break us out of poverty and move us to prosperity." As soon as he made the wish, he and his wife could hear the sound of animals outside. He walked out of the house and saw a thousand cattle on his farm! Overcome with gratitude, his heart filled with joy. For several days he felt as if he could walk on air.

However, a few days later, the farmer walked up a high hill to scout out where he would build a new barn. From the hill he looked over at his neighbor's land and couldn't believe what he saw. His neighbor, who had been as poor as he, had two thousand magnificent cattle roaming on his farm. In his joy over receiving the one thousand head of cattle, he completely forgot the angel's word that his neighbor would get a double portion of everything he received. When he compared his one thousand cattle with his neighbor's two thousand cattle, his herd seemed small and insignificant, and the thought sucked the joy right out of him. He went home in a foul mood, refused to eat dinner, and went to bed sulking. He could not fall asleep that night. In his mind all he could see was his neighbor's two thousand cattle. However, deep in the night, he remembered that the angel said he could make three wishes. So he began to forget about his neighbor's good fortune and started thinking about his second wish. It wasn't hard to decide what to wish for. He and his wife tried for years, unsuccessfully, to have a child. So he prayed a second time, "Gracious God, please give my wife and me a child." Soon thereafter his wife became pregnant.

For months the farmer felt overwhelming joy and gratitude. Finally, his wife delivered a healthy child. The next day, on the Sabbath, he went to the synagogue. When it came time for the prayers of the people, he stood up and shared his good news that a child, a son, had finally been born into his family. He barely sat down when his neighbor stood up and said, "God has been gracious to our little community. Just last night, my wife also gave birth—to twin sons. Thanks be to God!" After hearing the news, the farmer went home utterly dejected. Instead of being full of joy, envy filled his heart, and it would not go away. Finally, several days later, the farmer made his third request. He said, "Dear God, I ask that you strike me blind in one eye."

The legend ends with the angel of God coming back to the farmer and asking him why his heart was so full of vengeance. With pent-up rage the farmer said: "I cannot stand to see my neighbor get double what I get. I'll gladly sacrifice half of my vision for the satisfaction of knowing that my neighbor will never again be able to look at his two thousand cattle or his two sons." The angel sat silent for a long time. Finally, with a tear in his eye, the angel said: "O child of God, why have you turned an occasion for thanksgiving into a time of resentment and jealousy? Your third request will not be granted—not because the Lord lacks integrity but because God is full of mercy. You have brought sadness not only to yourself but to the very heart of God."

Let me give you a surefire formula for misery. Be like that farmer. Constantly compare what you have to what others have and then become resentful over it. Do that and I guarantee misery will be your lifetime companion. Why? Because no matter how many good things you have in your life, somebody else always has better. They have a better job, make more money, own a nicer house, are married to a more attractive spouse, have more successful children, enjoy better health, have a higher IQ, or are more popular. So if you want to be miserable, constantly compare what you have with those who have it better, then let envy and resentment fill your heart. On the other hand, if you want a surefire formula for happiness, then constantly notice all the wonderful gifts in your life and give thanks for them on a daily basis.

"Gratitude Saved My Life"

Not long ago I met a newly retired minister who lived out the legend of the poor farmer. Thankfully, he came to realize how bankrupt envy and resentment made his life, so he made a life-enriching shift to gratitude. I'd like to tell you his story.

At age twenty-five, when he graduated from seminary, his bishop appointed him to a small rural church with a small salary. However, he and his wife loved the congregation, the people loved them in return, and it proved a wonderful pastoral experience. This story continued for the next twenty years. He served several other churches, all small congregations with small salaries. But he loved his work and felt grateful to be a pastor. However, when he turned forty-five, he began to pay close attention to the back section of his state denominational journal. That's where they listed all the pastor salaries in his conference, from the highest to the lowest. He noticed that his salary fell slightly below the midpoint range. So he began to look at those above him. The more he looked, the worse he felt. He saw one man who made a higher salary and thought to himself: *I've been in ministry longer than he has. Why does he have a better appointment?* He saw another name and thought, *I'm a better preacher than he is, so why do I make less money?* This went on for five years. Every year when the new journal came out, he turned to the back section, compared where he was on the salary scale, and became more and more bitter.

By now he was fifty. All the gratitude and joy he had known earlier in his ministry disappeared. He became a jealous, bitter, joyless, resentful man. One night, when his wife and children left for an overnight trip, he had a profound spiritual experience. For the first time in several years, he looked in the mirror and saw what he had become, and he didn't like what he saw. That night, during his evening prayer, he confessed his bitterness and resentment and begged God to forgive him. He then walked to his desk, picked up his conference journal, tore out the salary section, and burned it in the wood-burning stove in his living room.

He then made a promise to God that he would once again be grateful for his pastoral appointment, his family, and the many other good things in his life. And he made good on that promise. From that day forward, for the next fifteen years before his retirement, this pastor began his day by thanking God for every good gift he could think of, including the great privilege of serving as a pastor, regardless of the church's size. He decided to quit complaining about what he didn't have, and he began expressing gratitude for what he did have, and it made a huge difference. He told me, "Even with the struggles—and I've had plenty—the past fifteen years have been the best years of my life." He then added, "I plan to continue giving thanks to God until the day I die." He concluded his story by saying, "Gratitude saved my life."

Giving Thanks in Spite Of

If space permitted, hundreds of biblical examples of gratitude could be listed. From the beginning of the Bible to the end, Scripture constantly challenges us to express thanksgiving. God knows that expressing gratitude is good for our mind, body, and soul, so God encourages us to practice the discipline of thanksgiving. However, for the purposes of this chapter, I'd like to focus our attention on giving thanks "in spite of." It's easy to give thanks when life is going well. It's more difficult to express thanks when we find ourselves struggling. However, during the hard times expressing gratitude is especially important.

We see that clearly in the life of David. For example, Psalm 57 is all about giving thanks in spite of bad circumstances. We don't know all the details, but David wrote this psalm during a particularly difficult period in his life. In the psalm he speaks of being surrounded by "destroying storms" (v. 1). We don't know all the storms he faced at that time. But we do know David felt under assault by his enemies. He wrote: "I lie down among lions that greedily devour human prey; their teeth are spears and arrows, their tongues sharp swords. . . . They set a net for my steps. . . . They dug a pit in my path" (57:4, 6).

Although the details are unclear, we know David faced enormous struggles when he wrote this psalm. He found himself in a hard, painful, and lonely place. And yet, in spite of his struggles, David practiced gratitude. In spite of the many "destroying storms" hammering him, David said: "I will give thanks to you, O Lord, among the peoples; I will sing praises to you among the nations. For your steadfast love is as high as the heavens; your faithfulness extends to the clouds. Be exalted, O God, above the heavens. Let your glory be over all the earth" (vv. 9–10). In spite of his struggles, David still gave thanks for God's steadfast love. In spite of all the storms David faced, he still expressed gratitude. David knew how to give thanks "in spite of." And that kind of gratitude helped give David the strength to carry on.

Giving thanks "in spite of" is what our Pilgrim forefathers and foremothers did back in 1621. You have heard many times how that little band of Puritans set out on the *Mayflower* and came to the new country. The first winter proved much worse than they anticipated. By April only 50 of the original 102 had survived. A discussion arose as to whether those remaining should give up and go back to the Old World, but they decided to stay and plant one more crop. When the first anniversary of their landing rolled around, discussion arose about how it should be observed. Some proposed a day of mourning when attention would be focused on all those who lay in graves in foreign soil. But the others said: "No, a day of thanksgiving would be more appropriate. After all, fifty of us have survived. We have gathered in a good harvest. The Indians have been our friends. Let's focus on what we have going for us, not on what we have going against us." Those early Pilgrims chose gratitude rather than resentment, and that was the birth of what we call Thanksgiving. And that spirit of giving thanks "in spite of" is what God calls us to do as followers of Jesus Christ.

However, I can hear the skeptics. Inevitably some of you are thinking: *You don't understand my situation. Horrible things are happening in my life. How can I be grateful?* That question reminds me of a story about an elderly English pastor known throughout his community for his pulpit prayers. He always managed to find something to thank God for, even in strained circumstances. One stormy Sunday morning, when everything was going poorly in the community and in the lives of many people, including the pastor, he stepped to the pulpit to pray. A member of the congregation thought to himself, *Our preacher will have nothing to thank God for on a wretched morning like this.* The old pastor began his prayer, "We thank Thee, O God, that it is not always like this."

Three Ways to Express Gratitude

Scientific research, the Bible, and life experience make clear that expressing gratitude leads to contentment. What follows are three practical strategies for doing so. I regularly practice these strategies in my own life and highly commend them to you.

The first strategy for expressing gratitude is to *pray gratitude prayers*. A good example can be found in the book of Philippians. In this letter Paul gives thanks to God for his dear friends at the church in Philippi. He says, "I thank my God every time I remember you, constantly praying with joy in every one of my prayers for all of you" (Phil. 1:3–4).

Author Anne Lamott once said that in the end there are only two prayers: "Help me, help me, help me," and "Thank you, thank you, thank you." I think she's on to something. We all have times in our life when the only prayer we can utter is, "Help me, help me, help me." But we must also remember to pray, "Thank you, thank you, thank you."

Many methods exist for praying prayers of gratitude. For example, every morning, when we first wake up, we can thank God for the gift of another day of life. During the day we can pray prayers of gratitude at mealtimes, thanking God for providing for us. I like to pray prayers of gratitude at the end of the day, as I lie in bed before falling asleep. I think back on the day and give thanks to God for the gifts of that day, both big and small, from laughter over lunch with a friend, to a special pastoral moment that occurred during the day, to the companionship of my spouse who lies beside me in the bed.

A second way to express gratitude is to *write gratitude letters*. Again, Philippians offers a good example. In this New Testament book, originally a letter from Paul to the church of Philippi, Paul says, "For even when I was in Thessalonica, you sent me aid more than once when I was in need. . . . The gifts you sent . . . are a fragrant offering . . . pleasing to God" (Phil. 4:16, 18 NIV). Paul literally wrote a letter to this church, thanking them for their support.

Psychologists have learned that when we write people gratitude letters, expressing thanks for something they did for us, it substantially boosts our happiness levels. We can write these gratitude letters to family members, friends, fellow church members, teachers, or anyone else who impacts our life in a positive way, big or small. Not only will writing gratitude letters or e-mails raise our happiness level; it will also be a blessing to those who receive them. I can personally attest to that. I often receive letters and e-mails from readers, expressing gratitude for a book or article I wrote, or from members of my congregation, thanking me for a sermon or other pastoral activity that helped them. Such letters are a huge gift and blessing in my life.

A third way to express gratitude is to *keep a gratitude journal*. Once more Paul's letter to the church in Philippi offers guidance for us. In the letter Paul encourages his readers to think about all the positive things we can give thanks for. He says, "Whatever is true, whatever is noble, whatever is right, whatever is pure, whatever is lovely, whatever is admirable—if anything is excellent or praiseworthy—think about such things" (Phil. 4:8 NIV).

Keeping a gratitude journal is a practical way to live out Paul's challenge to "think about such things." I can tell you from extensive personal experience that keeping a gratitude journal is a life-enriching discipline. I've kept a journal since high school, and it's one of the most important spiritual disciplines in my life—right up there with worship, prayer, Bible study, tithing, and service to others. I cannot overemphasize how important journaling is for me or how much it feeds my soul. My journal contains many things, including prayers, thoughts, insights, feelings, and interesting experiences of the day. But at heart it's a gratitude journal. Every evening I write down what I'm thankful for from the day, both big and small. This practice constantly builds contentment into my life.

A good bit of research has been done on the power of gratitude journals. For example, some years ago a psychologist did a fascinating study. Researchers studied a group of extremely depressed people, folks who had been diagnosed as "severely depressed." Some were so depressed they could barely leave their beds. All the depressed people in the study agreed to carry out a simple daily task. Every day they had to recall and write down three good things that happened that day. For example, "My daughter called to say hello." Or, "I read a chapter of a book my therapist recommended." Or, "The sun finally came out today." The results were amazing. Within fifteen days their depression lifted from "severely depressed" to "mildly or moderately depressed." In the end 94 percent of the people in the study experienced relief from their depression.[3]

Gratitude has healing power. It's one of the most helpful strategies available for increasing life contentment and happiness. Praying gratitude prayers, writing gratitude letters, and keeping a gratitude journal are three effective ways to live out this practice.

A Lesson in Gratitude from a Six-Year-Old at a Pizza Parlor

When my children were young, we lived in Nashville, Tennessee. Every Tuesday night my wife and two children and I went to Mr. Gatti's Pizza Parlor. Mr. Gatti's had an "all you can eat" buffet on Tuesday night and kids ate free. All four of us could eat dinner for eight dollars, quite a bargain. I always said that I went for the kids, but that's not true. The fact is I loved Mr. Gatti's! The pizza tasted great, they had an impressive salad bar, and they also provided a delicious dessert — baked pizza dough covered with butter, sugar, and cinnamon. What's not to like!

We ate at Mr. Gatti's every Tuesday night for a couple of years. Then one Tuesday evening, when we pulled into the parking lot, Mr. Gatti's appeared abandoned. We got out of the car and walked to the front door. At that point we realized that Mr. Gatti's had gone out of business. All the furniture was gone, and a "for sale" sign hung on the front door. We got back into the car, and I began moaning and groaning. "I can't believe Mr. Gatti's closed. This is the pits! I can't believe they closed down with no warning at all." On and on I bellyached. And then my six-year-old daughter, Laura, said something quite profound. She said, "I think that instead of being upset that Mr. Gatti's closed down, we should be grateful for all the times we came here and enjoyed it."

CHAPTER 9

CONTENTED PEOPLE CARE FOR THEIR BODIES

Do you not know that your bodies are temples of the Holy Spirit, who is in you, whom you have received from God? You are not your own; you were bought at a price. Therefore honor God with your bodies.
— 1 Corinthians 6:19–20 NIV

During my seminary years I heard an interesting presentation by Dr. Wayne Oates, an expert in pastoral care. During his lecture he spoke about "stewardship of the body." He said that while most religious leaders focus on people's spiritual souls, they also need to be concerned about people's physical bodies. Then Oates said: "You can do nothing more spiritual than to maintain your own physical health. Your body is the temple of the Holy Spirit. You serve God well if you take care of your body as a means of worshiping God." I've never forgotten those words. Throughout my ministerial career I've challenged my congregations, including myself, to care for our bodies as a means of serving and worshiping God.

Researchers have discovered two significant factors concerning the connection between physical health and happiness. On the one hand, people with physical challenges, including serious disabilities, can adapt to their limitations and still live a full and contented life. On the other hand, taking good care of our physical bodies is an important contributor to overall life satisfaction. For example, after citing clinical research showing that aerobic exercise proved as effective at treating depression as the antidepressant drug Zoloft, Lyubomirsky listed numerous benefits of physical activity. She then affirmed that "exercise may very well be the most effective instant happiness booster of all activities."[1]

Lyubomirsky concluded her comments about the value of physical fitness under the subtitle "Last Word" by saying: "No one in our society needs to be told that exercise is good for us. Whether you are overweight or have a chronic illness or are a slim couch potato, you've probably heard or read this dictum countless times throughout your life. But has anyone told you—indeed, *guaranteed* you—that regular physical activity will make you happier? I swear by it."[2]

The scientific research is clear. Taking good care of our physical bodies contributes to happiness and life satisfaction. And while stewardship of the body is not a major biblical theme, it is taught in Scripture. For example, in 1 Corinthians Paul says: "Do you not know that your bodies are temples of the Holy Spirit, who is in you, whom you have received from God? You are not your own; you were bought at a price. Therefore honor God with your bodies" (1 Cor. 6:19–20 NIV).

Dead Man Walking

A good example of God's concern for our physical bodies can be found in the story of the prophet Elijah in 1 Kings 19.

As we saw in chapter 3, the story begins with Elijah's sitting under a tree in the desert, depressed and burned out and ready to throw in the towel. If you follow the story, you learn that Elijah eventually recovered from his burnout and went back to work. One of the steps in his renewal involved physical restoration.

This biblical story about Elijah's renewal has profound relevance to Americans in the twenty-first century. As everyone knows by now, we have a health crisis in America today. A full 70 percent of American adults today are overweight or obese. This startling reality results in billions of dollars a year in health-care costs. It also contributes to high rates of heart disease, cancer, diabetes, and premature death. Sadly our children are following our example. A growing and alarming number of children in America are overweight or obese. It's getting so bad that many health experts predict that our children will live shorter lives than their parents. Clearly stewardship of our bodies is an important spiritual issue we seriously need to address.

All of which brings us back to Elijah's story of burnout to renewal in 1 Kings 19. Given Elijah's condition, it's interesting to see what God did *not* do. God did not preach a sermon to Elijah. God did not encourage Elijah to pray. God did not send Elijah to church. God did not refer Elijah to a counselor. What did God do? *God restored Elijah's physical body.* Elijah slept and ate. Then Elijah took a long walk. Elijah's journey from burnout to renewal included adequate sleep, healthy food, and vigorous exercise. Let's quickly review all three.

First, *Elijah got adequate sleep.* The text says, "Then he lay down under the broom tree and fell asleep . . . and lay down again" (vv. 5–6). The first thing Elijah did was sleep. Adequate sleep is absolutely necessary to good health. Unfortunately, many Americans do not get enough sleep. For example, many children in America routinely go to school sleepy, and insurance companies report that a growing number of automobile accidents are caused by lack of sleep. Millions of Americans are sleep deprived. Like Elijah we need to sleep and then sleep some more.

Second, *Elijah ate healthy food*. The text reads: "There at his head was a cake baked on hot stones, and a jar of water. He ate and drank. . . . He got up, and ate and drank" (vv. 6, 8). After sleeping, Elijah ate. And he didn't eat French fries and a cheeseburger. The Bible says he ate a "cake." At first glance that sounds pretty good. We get images of chocolate cake with icing. But this cake was baked whole-grain bread. In other words, God gave Elijah his Wheaties! And instead of drinking a Coke, Elijah drank water. This is a crucial issue. By and large Americans eat a terrible diet. I once heard a person say, "A lot of people are dying early deaths, killed by their own hands, if forks and spoons can be counted as weapons." If we want to get well or stay well, we need to eat a healthier diet.

Finally, *Elijah engaged in vigorous exercise*. The text says, "He went in the strength of that food forty days and forty nights to Horeb the mount of God" (v. 8). Elijah hiked for forty days on his way to Mount Horeb. On his journey from burnout to renewal, God led Elijah to participate in robust physical activity.

If we want to become healthy or stay healthy, we, like Elijah, must get adequate sleep; we must eat a balanced and nutritious diet; and we must get regular exercise. Doing so will make a huge difference in our lives. People who keep physically fit reduce their anxiety and stress, reduce their risk of disease, improve their sleep, protect against cognitive impairments as they age, control their weight, save significant amounts of money on medical expenses, and experience more happiness and contentment in their lives. Keeping fit is a huge factor in our overall quality of life.

Of course, we already know all of this. Everyone reading these words knows that we need to get adequate sleep, eat a healthy diet, and get regular exercise. The problem is not lack of information. The problem is lack of discipline. And New Year's resolutions and fad diets won't solve that problem. So how can we successfully maintain good health practices? The only way I know to do this is by making physical fitness a spiritual issue. We need to internalize the words of Scripture noted above: "Do you not know that your bodies are temples of the Holy Spirit, who is in you, whom you have received from God? You are not your own; you were bought at a price. Therefore honor God with your bodies" (1 Cor. 6:19–20 NIV). The NRSV goes even further, saying we should "glorify God" with our body.

The Bible teaches us that our bodies are the temple of God. We don't own our bodies; God does. And God expects us to take care of our bodies. That means Christians should not harm our bodies with tobacco, drugs, excessive alcohol, overeating, or poor eating habits. And it means we should care for our bodies by getting adequate sleep, eating a healthy diet, and getting regular exercise. This kind of thinking is the only way I know to maintain good health habits. Willpower alone is not enough. Instead, physical fitness needs to be seen as a spiritual priority.

As Christian believers, we are called by God to practice numerous spiritual disciplines. For example, Christians worship God on Sunday. Christians give of their financial resources to God's work. Christians pray. Christians read the Bible. Christians belong to a small group of Christian friends for mutual support and spiritual growth. We need to add to that list: Christians take care of their bodies. Not because we love eating broccoli or going to the gym. Most of us would far rather eat chocolate ice cream than broccoli, and most of us would rather sit in the recliner than go to the gym. But in order to please God, we eat broccoli and go to the gym anyway. Christians do these kinds of things because God expects us—indeed God requires us—to care for our bodies. So practicing good health habits is not about keeping a New Year's resolution or having strong willpower. Instead, stewardship of our bodies is an essential part of our Christian faith. When we make the connection between caring for our physical bodies and our Christian faith, we are far more likely to be faithful stewards of our bodies.

From Surfing to Sedentary to Stewardship

So far we've looked at what science and Scripture say about stewardship of the body. I'd now like to share some of my personal experience on this topic. Stewardship of the body first became a serious issue for me back in 1994. Before then I lived in Hawaii and was an avid surfer. Surfing is a physically demanding sport. It doesn't look like it in the movies. You see people standing on their boards, riding a wave, having a good time. What you don't see is that after you take that ride, you have to paddle back out to sea, against the waves, pounding your way through the surf, and it absolutely wears you out! Surfing kept me in great shape when I lived in Hawaii.

But then I moved from Honolulu to Nashville to begin PhD work at Vanderbilt University. Unfortunately, no good surfing spots exist in middle Tennessee! In that new setting I did not take care of my body. I ate a lot of fast food. Since a Burger King stood across the street from the Divinity School, a Whopper and fries became my routine lunch. Given the extreme demands of my doctoral studies and pastoral duties, I rationalized to myself that I didn't have time to exercise and became totally sedentary. Within several months my blood pressure shot up, I gained some weight, and I felt rotten. At that point God began to deal with me about poor stewardship of my body. I began to realize — not just in my head but also in my heart — that physical fitness was a spiritual issue. I realized that God wasn't just interested in my soul but also in my body. I realized that God had given me this body and God expected me to take care of it.

A few weeks later I went into the sanctuary of my church. In that quiet moment I knelt at the altar. I then promised God that with divine help I would take better care of my body — or more theologically accurate — I would take better care of God's body that God had loaned me. I made an oath, a sacred promise to God, that I would take seriously the biblical call to be a good steward of my body.

For over twenty years I have tried to live out that promise. I eat a fairly healthy diet. I exercise faithfully. And I get regular rest. I certainly don't do these three things perfectly. For example, I have a weakness for southern-style sweet iced tea, the sweeter the better. If I were God, sweet iced tea would lower your blood pressure, lower your cholesterol, lower your weight, and make you good-looking! I know that I don't need that extra sugar. I tried to quit once but really missed it. So I finally said: "I eat healthy. I exercise several times a week. I don't smoke. I don't drink. And I don't run around with other women. So if I want a glass of sweet tea at lunch, I'm going to drink it!" I've also been known to eat an occasional bowl of ice cream. So I'm certainly not perfect when it comes to diet. But because I believe my body is a temple of God and that God expects me to honor God with my body, I eat at least a somewhat healthy diet. It's a spiritual issue for me.

I also get regular exercise. I work out several times a week at the gym, at home, or on my bike. I'd like to tell you that I love exercising, that I can't wait to work out and get sweaty, but that would be a lie. When I come home from work, what I *want* to do is sit in my recliner and watch the evening news or read the paper. But because I believe my body is a temple of God and God expects me to honor God with my body, I force myself to work out. I made a pledge to God that I would exercise, so I do. Plus, I feel a lot better when I do.

Finally, I try to get adequate rest. I learned the hard way early in my career that working seven days a week is a recipe for burnout—physically, emotionally, vocationally, relationally, and spiritually. So I take time off. Since I work all day Sunday and half a day on Saturday, I take every Friday off. I also take all of my vacation every year. And you know what? The churches I've served never once died while I was on vacation. Somehow they manage to survive! And my guess is that your office or business will survive your being gone a few weeks a year on vacation. Although it's a cheesy statement, I try to live out the saying I once heard to "divert daily, withdraw weekly, and abandon annually." I highly commend it to you.

Over the past twenty years, I've learned that when I eat a reasonably healthy diet, get regular exercise, and get adequate rest, I am a better pastor, husband, father, friend, person, and Christian. The key, at least for me, is framing this as a spiritual issue. When we become convinced—not just in our head but in our heart—that taking care of our bodies is a spiritual issue, we will find ways, even with our busy schedules, to keep more physically fit. And the good news is that it is never too late. Health experts have learned that people in their seventies and eighties and even in their nineties can greatly benefit from proper diet, age-appropriate exercise, and adequate rest. So it's never too late to begin.

Getting Started

Practicing stewardship of the body remains a huge challenge for most people, including me. No silver bullet exists

to become and stay physically fit. However, the following
five steps can help us make progress.

1. *Remember the positives*. Caring for our bodies by getting
   adequate rest, eating a healthy diet, and getting regular exercise provides enormous benefits: physical,
   emotional, and even financial. Being a physically fit
   person also significantly increases life satisfaction and
   contentment.
2. *Start small*. A simple walking regimen for example,
   provides huge health benefits and doesn't require any
   equipment (other than a comfortable pair of walking
   shoes) or even a membership at a gym.
3. *Join others*. Exercising with another person or a group
   of people will help motivate you to continue your regimen. It's also a lot more fun. When it comes to exercise,
   Ecclesiastes is correct: "Two are better than one."
4. *Frame it as a spiritual issue*. Remember the words of
   Wayne Oates: "You can do nothing more spiritual than
   to maintain your own physical health. Your body is the
   temple of the Holy Spirit. You serve God well if you take
   care of your body as a means of worshiping God." And
   remember the words of Scripture, "Do you not know
   that your bodies are temples of the Holy Spirit, who is
   in you, whom you have received from God? You are not
   your own; you were bought at a price. Therefore honor
   God with your bodies" (1 Cor. 6:19–20 NIV).
5. *Just do it*. In the end, when it comes to getting adequate
   rest, eating a nutritious diet, and getting exercise, we
   finally have to gut it out and, in the words of Nike,
   "Just do it." A few years ago I read a book by a woman
   named Nancy Beach. In a section on exercise she said:
   "To be honest, I've been exercising regularly for over
   twenty-five years, and I'm still waiting to actually like it.
   I never experience the rush or the high that some people

promise. I never wake up in the morning excited to put on my running shoes. I just have to do it. It's a decision I've already made, and I don't give myself permission to miss except on Sundays, or if I'm really sick."[3]

One Car to Last a Lifetime

I once heard a friend give a speech at a Kiwanis Club meeting. She used an analogy I've never forgotten. She asked her audience to imagine that every person in America, when they turned sixteen, got a brand-new, high-quality car. But it came with a catch. That car would be the only car they would ever get. That car had to last their entire lifetime — fifty, sixty, maybe seventy years. She said if that were the case, people would take incredible care of their one and only car. They would change the oil regularly, keep it clean, and maintain it carefully. Then she made the connection to our bodies. When we are born, she said, we are given a wonderful body. But it comes with a catch. That body is the only one we'll ever receive. It has to last a lifetime. Therefore, we need to take good care of it. My friend is correct. God gave us a wonderful body. But it has to last a lifetime. Therefore, God calls us to take good care of our bodies as a spiritual discipline.

CHAPTER 10

CONTENTED PEOPLE CARE FOR THEIR SOULS

Remember your creator. . . . Fear God, and keep his commandments; for that is the whole duty of everyone.

— Ecclesiastes 12:1, 13

About a year before George Harrison died in 2001, I heard an interesting interview on the radio about the former Beatle. During the interview George talked about his life, including his experience with the Beatles. He said that when they first started out, "it was all about the fame." And of course, the Beatles accumulated more fame than they ever dreamed of having. However, the excitement of the fame finally wore off. After that, said George, "it was all about the money." And my goodness, they made a lot of money! But in the end fame and money did not satisfy George Harrison. "At this point in my life," said George, "it's all about finding God."

What an interesting comment. First, it was all about fame. Then it was all about money. Then it was all about God.

When that interview occurred, George had been fighting cancer for several years. When mortality became real to him, spiritual issues became even more crucial. I'm not saying George Harrison was a Christian believer. But eventually, after fame and fortune disappointed, as it always will, finding God became a crucial factor in his quest to live a substantial and contented life.

Throughout this book we have explored what science, Scripture, and experience teach about life satisfaction and contentment. So far we've seen that:

- Contented people know that external circumstances don't determine happiness.
- Contented people use trials as growth opportunities.
- Contented people cultivate optimism.
- Contented people focus on the present.
- Contented people practice forgiveness.
- Contented people practice generosity.
- Contented people nurture relationships.
- Contented people express gratitude.
- Contented people care for their bodies.

In this final chapter we'll learn that contented people also care for their souls. In short, affirming and practicing faith lead to a more contented life. When it comes to the topic of religious faith, science and Scripture once again concur. Both scientific research and the Bible tell us that people of faith are happier and more content than people without religious faith. One final time let's hear from several experts in the field of positive psychology.

- "One of the most robust findings of happiness research" is that "people who believe in God are happier." —Richard Layard, *Happiness*[1]

- Religious people are "happier and more satisfied with life than nonreligious people." — Martin Seligman, *Authentic Happiness*[2]
- Religious people, compared to nonreligious people, are healthier, live longer, have stronger social support, cope better with trauma, see more purpose in life, have stronger self-esteem, experience more joy and awe, and feel more satisfied and hopeful. "Religious people are happier, healthier, and recover better after traumas than nonreligious people," and "scientists can no longer ignore the powerful influences of spirituality and religion on health and well-being." — Sonja Lyubomirsky, *The How of Happiness*[3]

A Tale of Two Funerals

In my line of work, I officiate at a good number of funerals. For some reason they seem to come in clusters. I may go a month or two without a funeral, and then two or three come close together. A few years ago I had two funerals back-to-back, one on a Monday afternoon and another on a Tuesday morning. Given their close proximity and the marked contrast between them, I still vividly remember the two services.

On Monday I led the funeral of a man with no church affiliation. His sister, a member of my congregation, asked me to do the funeral. He was clearly a good man who worked hard his entire life and loved his wife and children. However, he had no religious connection. As far as anyone knew, he had no faith at all. At the funeral I affirmed his life, including his hard work and love of family. However, the service lacked substance. Given his lack of religious faith, the family felt it would be hypocritical to have a traditional Christian funeral. So we did not sing the great hymns of faith, affirm the Apostles' Creed, or pray the Lord's Prayer. The service contained no resurrection hope, no celebration of faith, no connection with a Christian community, and no real joy. I did not make any judgment about this man's spiritual condition. That's God's job, not mine. After my comments, a friend of the deceased man spoke, along with a family member. Then we listened to a recording of a secular song he loved, and I concluded with a prayer for the family. Given the circumstances, the funeral went fine. But at least to me, it felt flat. As far as I could tell, this man lived a totally secular life, with no sense of transcendence or ultimate reality. Since faith had not been part of this man's life, it was not part of his death or part of his funeral. As a result, the funeral service felt impoverished. I left the funeral home that afternoon with a heavy heart.

The next morning I officiated at another funeral, this time for an elderly man in my congregation. In some ways the two men shared similarities. They both lived to their late eighties, and both men worked hard and loved their families. But the second funeral proved dramatically different. The second man put faith at the center of his life. He loved God and his church, and we deeply loved him. We cried some at his funeral, but we also laughed. Mostly we affirmed our common faith. We sang the great hymns, we read Holy Scripture, we affirmed the Apostles' Creed, we prayed the Lord's Prayer, and we celebrated Holy Communion, looking forward to that day when we would be reunited with our beloved friend around God's great banquet table in heaven. I cannot overstate the radical difference between the two funerals. What set them apart was simple and yet profound. One man neglected God, and the other man put God at the center of his life. And that made a huge difference in the way they lived, the way they died, and how they were memorialized.

Benefits of Faith

We've already noted that scientific research indicates that religious faith increases life satisfaction and happiness. Obviously the Bible agrees with this conclusion. An entire book could be written on this subject with hundreds of biblical examples. However, for our purposes, we'll focus on just one short example, the New Testament book of Philippians, which we've already looked at in previous chapters.

As noted earlier, the apostle Paul wrote the letter to the Philippians during a prison stay. In spite of his difficult circumstances, Paul said: "I have learned to be content whatever the circumstances. I know what it is to be in need, and I know what it is to have plenty. I have learned the secret of being content in any and every situation" (4:11–12 NIV). In spite of being in jail, Paul experienced well-being. Not a shallow or superficial kind of happiness but a deep sense of inner satisfaction, peace, and contentment. How is it possible to be content in a jail cell? The short answer is faith. Paul's abiding faith in God and Jesus Christ gave him the ability to experience life satisfaction and contentment even in trying circumstances. A careful review of Philippians reveals at least eight benefits of religious faith:.

1. Paul's faith gave him *courage in the face of fear*. He said, "I eagerly expect and hope that I will in no way be ashamed, but will have sufficient courage so that now as always Christ will be exalted in my body, whether by life or by death" (1:20 NIV). At the time Paul found himself in deep trouble with the Roman government. He did not know if he would be executed or freed or if he would spend the rest of his life in prison. His faith gave him courage to face that substantial fear.
2. Paul's faith gave him *joy in spite of difficulties*. He said, "Rejoice in the Lord always. I will say it again: Rejoice!"

(4:4 NIV). Even in prison Paul experienced deep joy—joy rooted in his relationship with God and the people of God.

3. Paul's faith gave him *a purpose bigger than himself.* He said, "I press on toward the goal to win the prize for which God has called me" (3:14 NIV). Paul felt a sense of purpose bigger than his own narrow self-interest. Instead, he lived to love and serve God and God's church.

4. Paul's faith gave him *friendships that encouraged and sustained him.* He said: "I thank my God every time I remember you. . . . I have you in my heart. . . . I long for all of you with the affection of Christ Jesus" (1:3, 7–8 NIV). Paul held close friendships among the people at the church in Philippi. Friendships in that community of faith enriched his life immensely and helped sustain him through tough times.

5. Paul's faith gave him *peace even in the midst of turmoil.* He said, "And the peace of God, which transcends all understanding, will guard your hearts and your minds in Christ Jesus" (4:7 NIV). Even in jail Paul trusted God, and that trust gave him a sense of internal peace and security in spite of inevitable human anxiety.

6. Paul's faith gave him *strength to face difficult circumstances.* He said, "I can do all this through him [Christ] who gives me strength" (4:13 NIV). Paul believed that God walked with him, and that sense of divine presence gave him the spiritual strength to face whatever came his way.

7. Paul's faith gave him *grace to accept himself as a beloved child of God.* He said, "Grace and peace to you from God our Father and the Lord Jesus Christ" (1:2 NIV). In a world that determines our worth primarily by appearance, affluence, and achievement, Paul rooted his self-worth in being a child of God, who, like a good father or mother, deeply loves, affirms, and accepts God's children.

8. Paul's faith gave him *hope for life beyond death*. He said, "[Christ] will transform our lowly bodies so that they will be like his glorious body" (3:21 NIV). Paul knew that he might be executed by the authorities at any time. And if the government didn't get him, illness or old age eventually would. But his faith gave him the ability to face death with hope—hope rooted in the resurrection of Jesus Christ.

Although many other benefits of faith could be listed, the point is clear: Affirming faith in God and Jesus Christ enriches our life in profound ways and promotes life satisfaction and contentment.

Beyond Bumper-Sticker Faith

However, I need to communicate clearly that I'm not talking about some kind of simplistic, happy-go-lucky faith that always smiles and says everything is wonderful if you love Jesus. I used to think of faith in these kinds of simplistic ways. When I was a teenager and a new Christian, I plastered my faith all over my old Buick convertible. On my rear bumper I had a sign that said, "God Is Alive." On my radio I had a sticker that said, "I'm hooked on Jesus." On my glove box I had a magnet that said, "God said it, I believe it, that settles it."

But that was a long time ago. My faith isn't so simple anymore. Bumper-sticker theology isn't enough these days. Why? Because I've preached too many hard funerals, including ones for children, youth, and young parents. I've seen too many broken dreams. I've prayed with too many cancer patients. I've seen too many terrors of the world. My faith today has a lot of ambiguity and unknowns. It has a lot of mystery. Faith is not always black-and-white and simple and easy. Sometimes faith is hard. One of my favorite verses in the whole Bible is "[Lord] I believe; help my unbelief" (Mark 9:24).

These days I can relate to Barbara Brown Taylor's words, "I cannot say for sure when my reliable ideas about God began to slip away, but the big chest I used to keep them in is smaller than a shoebox now."[4] Most honest Christians will admit having such feelings, at least sometimes. I certainly do. I don't pretend to have all the answers about God and faith. And yet, at the core of my being, I am a person of faith. In spite of doubts and unanswered questions, I know that God is alive and that I belong to God. I do believe, and that faith makes all the difference in the world.

Faith Practices

Faith practices, and not just faith beliefs, contribute to our contentment as believers. People do not experience life satisfaction just because they believe certain theological precepts about God and Jesus Christ. They also gain contentment from practicing faith disciplines like worship, prayer, Bible reading, service, practicing forgiveness, and connecting to a faith community. So, if we want our faith to make us happier, then we need to actively engage in faith practices. Twelve examples of historic spiritual disciplines that lead to a more contented life follow:

1. *Prayer*—communicating with God
2. *Silence*—being still and quiet before God
3. *Scripture*—reading and listening for God's voice through the Bible
4. *Fasting*—forfeiting meals for short periods of time for spiritual purposes

5. *Worship*—praising God who is worthy of our adoration and worship
6. *Giving*—financially supporting God's work in the world
7. *Service*—helping others in practical ways in the name of Christ
8. *Communion*—a tangible reminder that we are beloved children of God
9. *Journaling*—capturing on paper thoughts about our faith
10. *Justice*—actively seeking justice, especially for the poor and marginalized
11. *Sabbath*—dedicating one day per week for worship and rest
12. *Community*—connecting to other Christians for support and insight

Remember Your Creator

On several occasions in previous chapters, we explored passages from the book of Ecclesiastes. It seems appropriate, therefore, that we conclude by making one final trip to that book. As noted earlier, the writer of Ecclesiastes spent his entire adult life on a quest, seeking to discover the secrets of a good life. Ecclesiastes ends by telling readers to affirm faith in God. In the final words of the book, Ecclesiastes says, "Remember your creator. . . . The end of the matter; all has been heard. Fear God, and keep his commandments; for that is the whole duty of everyone" (12:1, 13).

Ecclesiastes' admonition to remember our Creator and affirm faith in God reminds me of a story that I'd like to share with you. The story comes from one of my heroes, Fred Craddock, a recently deceased pastor, teacher, and author.

As a young man, Fred served a small church in a tiny town of about 450 people called Custer, Oklahoma. The town included four churches and a café. On Sunday morning, people gathered at the four churches for worship and Sunday school. The best attendance in town on Sunday morning, however, could be found at the café. A group of men drove their pickup trucks to the café every Sunday morning where they drank coffee and discussed weather, cattle, and crops while their wives and children went to one of the four churches. Once in a while the café congregation lost a member because his wife finally got to him, or maybe his kids did. So, from time to time, one of the men would go off sheepishly to one of the churches.

These were not bad men. Instead, they were good men, family men, hardworking men. But they didn't have much interest in faith or church or religion. The patron saint of the group at the café was a man in his mid-seventies named Frank. Frank, a good and strong man, worked as a rancher, farmer, and cattleman. All the men at the café looked up to Frank. He served as the unofficial leader of the café congregation. They all said, "Old Frank will never go to church."

One day Fred Craddock met Frank on the street. Frank knew Fred was a preacher. When they met, Frank said to Fred, "I work hard, and I take care of my family, and I mind my own business." In short, he told Fred, "Leave me alone. I'm not a prospect for your church." Over the next couple of years, Frank repeated that same line to Fred several times, "I work hard, I take care of my family, and I mind my own business." Frank clearly was not interested in church. So Fred did not bother Frank.

That's why Fred, along with his congregation, the entire town, and especially the men at the café were so surprised when Frank, at age seventy-seven, came to church one Sunday, affirmed his faith in Jesus Christ, and asked to be baptized. The next week Fred baptized Frank. The men at the café speculated that Frank must be sick, that he felt scared to meet his Maker. Some said he must have heart trouble or something; he must be frightened. All kinds of stories circulated around town about why Frank got religion.

The day after Fred baptized Frank, the two of them got together for coffee. Fred said, "Frank, do you remember that little saying you used to say to me so much? 'I work hard, I take care of my family, and I mind my own business.'"

Frank said, "Yes, I remember. I said that a lot."

Fred said, "Do you still say that?"

Frank said, "Yes, I do."

So Fred said, "Then what's the difference?"

Frank said, "I didn't know then what my business was."[5]

Frank, at seventy-seven years old, finally discovered what his business was. Like the writer of Ecclesiastes, late in his life Frank came to realize that his business was to remember his Creator, to fear God, and to keep his commandments.

CONCLUSION

Several months ago I watched again the movie *The Prince of Tides*, staring Nick Nolte and Barbra Streisand. *The Prince of Tides* tells the story of a high school teacher and football coach named Tom Wingo who lost his joy, both vocationally and personally, but then found it again. The beginning of the movie finds Tom struggling with unemployment, burnout, and serious marital problems. However, after a long and painful process of healing, Tom reunites with his wife and children, returns to his vocation, and finds renewed contentment in his life. In the final scene of the film, we see Tom mowing the grass of his high school football field. In voice-over narration Tom says, "I am a teacher and a coach and a well-loved man—and it is more than enough."

Like Tom in *The Prince of Tides*, we are all broken in some ways, and sometimes we lose our joy. However, by engaging in the ten practices laid out in this book—practices confirmed by science, Scripture, and experience—we, like Tom, can find renewed contentment in our lives. In short, if we will:

- affirm that external circumstances don't determine happiness,

- use trials as growth opportunities,
- cultivate optimism,
- focus on the present,
- practice forgiveness,
- practice generosity,
- nurture relationships,
- express gratitude,
- take care of our bodies, and
- take care of our souls,

then we, like Tom in *The Prince of Tides*, will be able to say, "It is more than enough."

GUIDE FOR STUDY
AND REFLECTION

This guide is intended to help a leader in a small group setting explore and discuss *Searching for Happiness*, by Martin Thielen, or to help individuals reflect on the contents. Each week contains a Scripture verse to open a study session or devotional time, several questions for study or reflection, and a challenge for each individual to reflect on during the week.

You may want to divide each session into three sections, to help draw your participants into deep discussion and send them out equipped to reflect on what authentic contentment might look like for their lives.

1. *Getting Started.* Begin each session with a brief summary of the week's topic and Scripture passage. If participants have not read the chapter, you may want to assign a key section for someone to read aloud during this time.
2. *Reading and Responding.* Spend the bulk of each session discussing the Scripture passage and questions for that week.
3. *Reflecting on Contentment.* Close each session by reading the Challenge question for the week and then previewing the next chapter in the book. If you have time, you may want to ask if anyone has any initial reactions to the Challenge.

Depending on the length of your group's time together, you can spend more or less time on each section. The following time allotments are only a guide; adapt or ignore them based on the flow and fruitfulness of your group's discussion (see also "Tips for Group Leaders," p. 159). Always feel free to linger or move on to a new question as you sense topics resonating (or not) with your group.

	45-minute session	60-minute session	90-minute session
Getting Started	10 min.	15 min.	20 min.
Reading and Responding	30 min.	35 min.	60 min.
Reflecting on Contentment	5 min.	10 min.	10 min.

Chapter 1

Contented People Know That External Circumstances Don't Determine Happiness

*I kept my heart from no pleasure. . . . I . . . had great possessions. . . .
I made great works. . . . Then I considered all that my hands had done
and the toil I had spent in doing it, and again, all was vanity and a
chasing after wind.*

— Ecclesiastes 2:10, 7, 4, 11

1. Looking at your life from the outside, would people say you "should" be happy? Would such external assessments be right or wrong?

   _____

   _____

   _____

2. What external things do you often think would make you happier? A better job? A nicer house? Better health?

   _____

   _____

   _____

3. Which "path" from Ecclesiastes do you identify with the most? Are you most tempted to pursue the path of philosophy, the path of pleasure, the path of possessions, or the path of production?

   _____

   _____

   _____

4. In the preface, the author tells a story about a successful, affluent, and attractive woman named Sarah who asked, "If money, success, and beauty don't make you happy, what does?" If someone asked you that question, how would you respond?

_____

_____

_____

5. In our culture, we highly value appearance, affluence, and achievement. One person has called these "The three A's of American values." Why do you think these three traits are so important to us?

to feel free, in control } _selfish_

to be liked / respected } _motives_

_____

6. Positive psychologists claim that external circumstances like beauty, money, and career success account for only 10 percent of a person's overall happiness and contentment. Why is that finding so hard for most Americans to accept?

_____

_____

_____

Challenge: Imagine if all the external positives in your life were stripped away (a natural disaster strikes, for example, destroying your home, killing your loved ones, and leaving you permanently injured). Do you think you could find a way to be happy nonetheless? How?

_____

_____

_____

_____

_____

_____

Chapter 2

Contented People Use Trials as Growth Opportunities

Consider it pure joy, my brothers and sisters, whenever you face trials of many kinds, because you know that the testing of your faith produces perseverance. Let perseverance finish its work so that you may be mature and complete, not lacking anything.

—James 1:2–4 NIV

1. What is the greatest trial you have experienced? Would your response be characterized as surviving, recovering, or thriving?

   _____

   _____

   _____

2. How do you approach smaller trials in life? Do small setbacks leave you feeling devastated, mildly frustrated, or eager to overcome?

   _____

   _____

   _____

3. From what situation might you need to "pick the fruit and burn the rest"? What are the fruits to save, and what memories or emotions need to be burned?

   _____

   _____

   _____

4. If you were asked to give a speech to your church or civic organization on growing from adversity, what would you say?

_____

_____

_____

5. Think of a past or current trial in your life. How can you use that experience to help others?

_____

_____

_____

6. Whom do you personally know who used a life trial as an opportunity of growth? What can be learned from their experience?

_____

_____

_____

Challenge: Reach out to someone who has gone through or is currently going through a similar situation to what you are currently experiencing. What can you learn from this person? What can you offer that might help this person?

_____

_____

_____

_____

_____

_____

Chapter 3

Contented People Cultivate Optimism

Finally, brothers and sisters, whatever is true, whatever is noble, whatever is right, whatever is pure, whatever is lovely, whatever is admirable—if anything is excellent or praiseworthy—think about such things.

—Philippians 4:8 NIV

1. What seems to be your natural level of optimism? Do you easily identify "what went well" or "what is left" in a difficult circumstance?

   _____

   _____

   _____

2. What situations in your life (past or present) might be different if you approached them with a positive attitude, looking for and expecting to find good things there?

   _____

   _____

   _____

3. If cultivating optimism is both an act of discipline and an act of faith, which is harder for you? Is it more challenging to work at thinking positively or to have confidence in God's power to make things right?

   _____

   _____

   _____

4. In the story about Bob Dole found in the section, "'You Must Think about What You Have Left,'" Dole's doctor told him he must avoid thinking so much "about what you have lost. You must think about what you have left . . . and what you can do with it." What is your initial response to that story?

_____

_____

_____

5. Proverbs 17:22 says, "A cheerful heart is a good medicine, but a downcast spirit dries up the bones." What does that mean to you? Can you think of examples where this verse proved true in your own experience?

_____

_____

_____

6. See the section in chapter 3 called "Things I Have Not Lost." If you were going to write a list of things you have not lost, what would you write down?

_____

_____

_____

Challenge: For a whole day, try to approach every instance, from a paper cut to an unexpectedly high utility bill, with a positive attitude. Notice how you feel at the end of the day. Then try it for a whole week.

_____

_____

_____

_____

_____

_____

Chapter 4

Contented People Focus on the Present

So don't be anxious about tomorrow. God will take care of your tomorrow too. Live one day at a time.

—Matthew 6:34 TLB

1. Are you more often tempted to focus on the past or the future? Does this keep you from fully enjoying the present?

   _____

   _____

   _____

2. When is the last time you enjoyed a simple pleasure or celebrated "just because"?

   _____

   _____

   _____

3. Ecclesiastes emphasizes that all of us will one day die. How does reflecting on that fact affect your thinking about the way you live now? What if you had only one year left to live?

   _____

   _____

   _____

4. In Matthew 6:33 (TLB) Jesus says, "So don't be anxious about tomorrow. God will take care of your tomorrow too. Live one day at a time." Do you think it is possible to live like this? Why or why not?

   _____

   _____

   _____

5. Read Jeremiah 29:4–7. In this text, the prophet Jeremiah encouraged the exiles to make the best of their current life in Babylon rather than dwell on the past or the future. What might this text mean for us today in our context?

_____

_____

_____

6. Read the section in chapter 4 called, "The Best Time of My Life." How can we foster that kind of attitude in our own life?

_____

_____

_____

Challenge: Throw a party sometime in the next seven days. It could be as simple as using the good china and having a nice dessert with family dinner or as involved as inviting friends and decorating the house. How does taking time for fun and togetherness change the way you feel the rest of the week?

_____

_____

_____

_____

_____

_____

Chapter 5

Contented People Practice Forgiveness

Forgive us our sins, as we also forgive everyone who sins against us.
—Luke 11:4 NIV

1. What is the worst thing that has ever been done to you by another person? Have you forgiven that person? Are there any wrongs you have not forgiven?

   _____

   _____

   _____

2. Do you agree that forgiveness is more about work than faith? What would help you do that hard work of forgiveness?

   _____

   _____

   _____

3. Have you seen the "curved sword" of unforgiveness in action? How can refusing to forgive hurt you more than it hurts the person who wronged you?

   _____

   _____

   _____

4. In this chapter the author speaks about the costs of unforgiveness. What are some of the costs of refusing to forgive people who harm us?

   _____

   _____

   _____

5. Review the section in chapter 5 called, "Forgiveness Principles." Briefly review all five of them. Which of the five do you most resonate with? Why?

_____

_____

_____

6. Read the closing story, "I Remember Forgetting That." What feelings or thoughts does that story evoke in you?

_____

_____

_____

Challenge: Take steps to work on forgiving someone you need to forgive. Try praying for that person regularly or using Seligman's REACH process.

_____

_____

_____

_____

_____

_____

Chapter 6

Contented People Practice Generosity

A generous person will be enriched, and one who gives water will get water.

—Proverbs 11:25

1. What emotions do you associate with giving to others? Guilt? Duty? Joy?

   _____

   _____

   _____

2. How have you seen a person's kindness toward others heal his or her own pain? Has giving to others ever brought you through a difficult time or lifted you up on a rough day?

   _____

   _____

   _____

3. What is the most generous gift you have ever given? Think about what it cost you in terms of money, time, or personal sacrifice. How did it make you feel to give such a gift?

   _____

   _____

   _____

4. Read Proverbs 11:24–25 and Acts 20:35. What do these two passages mean to you?

   _____

   _____

   _____

5. Read the section, "Finding Joy at Walgreens." Have you ever participated in a "random act of kindness"? If so, share your experience with the group and how it made you feel.

_____

_____

_____

6. Karl Menninger was once asked, "What would you advise a person to do if he or she felt a nervous break-down coming on?" He replied, "If a person feels a ner-vous breakdown coming, they should lock up their house, go across the railway track, find someone in need, and do something to help that person." What do you think he meant by that?

_____

_____

_____

Challenge: Do the math to see what it would look like to tithe (give 10 percent of) not just your income but your time. What would it take to make that happen? What might be the result?

_____

_____

_____

_____

_____

_____

Chapter 7

Contented People Nurture Relationships

*Two are better than one, because they have a good return for their
labor: If either of them falls down, one can help the other up.*
— Ecclesiastes 4: 9–10 NIV

1. Thinking of the jar metaphor early in the chapter, does
   your life or your schedule have enough room in it for
   the "big rocks" of relationships? Are relationships your
   "biggest rocks," or does something else come first?

   _____

   _____

   _____

2. Is loneliness or relational strife a challenge to your happiness? What can you do to build deeper relationships
   or heal those that are strained?

   _____

   _____

   _____

3. What benefits have relationships brought to your life?
   Are these benefits different during difficult times than
   during peaceful times?

   _____

   _____

   _____

4. Find the paragraph about Will Miller's book, *Refrigerator Rights* under the section, "'Two Are Better than One.'" You will find a list of seven reasons why Miller believes many Americans are lonely. What is your response to this list? Do you think Miller is on target?

_____

_____

_____

5. Under the section "What Would Jesus Do?," we learn that Jesus nurtured both individual relationships and a group relationship. What steps can we take to better follow Christ's example of relationship building in our own life?

_____

_____

_____

6. Read the closing story under "Someone's Hand to Hold." What feelings does that story evoke in you?

_____

_____

_____

Challenge: Make a list of all the significant people in your life: family members, old friends, new friends, neighbors, and coworkers. Try to reach out to one person every day with a note, quick conversation, or act of kindness. After a month, look back and see how your relationships may have improved.

_____

_____

_____

_____

_____

_____

Chapter 8

Contented People Express Gratitude

Give thanks in all circumstances; for this is God's will for you.
— 1 Thessalonians 5:18 NIV

1. Have you ever let envy, resentment, or comparison rob you of joy? What is the result?

   _____

   _____

   _____

2. Name five things you are grateful for. How does thinking of these things make you feel about your life in this moment? Do you notice changes to your breathing, your expression, or your attitude?

   _____

   _____

   _____

3. When you pray, does the "help me!" or the "thank you!" tend to come first? Are your struggles or blessings more on top of your mind throughout the day?

   _____

   _____

   _____

4. In this chapter, happiness expert Dr. Sonja Lyubomirsky is quoted as saying, "The expression of gratitude is a kind of metastrategy for achieving happiness." What do you think she meant by this statement?

   _____

   _____

   _____

5. In 1 Thessalonians 5:18 Paul tells us to "Give thanks in all circumstances." How is that possible? Can you give examples of "giving thanks in all circumstances" from your own life?

_____

_____

_____

6. Of the three methods for expressing gratitude mentioned in this chapter — praying gratitude prayers, writing gratitude letters, and keeping a gratitude journal — which one most resonates with you and why?

_____

_____

_____

Challenge: Keep a gratitude journal for at least a week. Every morning, write ten new things you feel grateful for. Notice how this activity shifts your focus for the day to come.

_____

_____

_____

_____

_____

_____

Chapter 9

Contented People Care for Their Bodies

Do you not know that your bodies are temples of the Holy Spirit, who is in you, whom you have received from God? You are not your own; you were bought at a price. Therefore honor God with your bodies.
— 1 Corinthians 6:19–20 NIV

1. Do you see a connection between your physical and spiritual health? How so? Does physical activity make you feel happier?

   _____

   _____

   _____

2. Do any challenges to your physical health affect your happiness? Do you have problems sleeping? Do you lack energy for the things you want to do? Do you struggle with discipline when it comes to good eating and exercise habits? What can you do to improve these aspects of your health?

   _____

   _____

   _____

3. How might a "stewardship" perspective on physical health, believing that your body is on loan from God, change the way you approach the care of your body?

   _____

   _____

   _____

4. In the introduction of this chapter, Dr. Wayne Oates is quoted as saying, "You can do nothing more spiritual than to maintain your own physical health. Your body is the temple of the Holy Spirit. You serve God well if you take care of your body as a means of worshiping God." What is your response to that quote?

_____

_____

_____

5. In this chapter the author mentions the advice to "divert daily, withdraw weekly, and abandon annually." What do you think about this threefold plan for carving out rest in our life? What would this look like for your schedule?

_____

_____

_____

6. Read the final story, "One Car to Last a Lifetime." What thoughts come to mind as you hear this story?

_____

_____

_____

Challenge: Pray about your physical health and make a commitment to God to start a new, healthier practice. Pray daily to remember that this is not just a wise thing to do, but a spiritual discipline.

_____

_____

_____

_____

_____

_____

Chapter 10

Contented People Care for Their Souls

Remember your creator. . . . Fear God, and keep his commandments;
for that is the whole duty of everyone.

—Ecclesiastes 12:1, 13

1. Religious involvement has many benefits: community, purpose, comfort. Would you also say your faith makes you happier? Why or why not?

   _____

   _____

   _____

2. How do you feel about mystery, doubt, or ambiguity in your faith? Does such complexity cause you anxiety or enhance your appreciation for a big, uncontainable God?

   _____

   _____

   _____

3. How does practicing your faith bring happiness in a way that simply believing does not?

   _____

   _____

   _____

4. In this chapter author Richard Layard is quoted as saying, "One of the most robust findings of happiness research" is that "people who believe in God are happier." Do you agree with that affirmation? Why or why not?

   _____

   _____

   _____

5. In the section "Benefits of Faith," the author lists eight benefits of faith that Paul affirms in the book of Philippians. Quickly review all eight. Which do you most resonate with? Why?

_____

_____

_____

6. Read the closing story about the seventy-seven-year-old man named Frank who affirmed faith late in his life. What thoughts or feelings does that story evoke in you?

_____

_____

_____

Challenge: Think through the list of twelve spiritual practices on pages 128 and 129 and identify those that have the greatest effect on your sense of joy and contentment. Find ways to engage in those practices on a weekly, if not daily, basis.

_____

_____

_____

_____

_____

_____

Tips for Group Leaders

- Be aware of group dynamics and how much time is actually available for the study. Does your group tend to trickle in over the first fifteen minutes of class? Is it customary to end early to allow time for prayer concerns or socializing? If your group is being newly formed for this study, set the schedule and tone that will enable a fruitful discussion and experience for all.
- Distribute copies of *Searching for Happiness* at least a week before the first session.
- As you prepare to lead each session, read the questions and challenge for the week, the corresponding book chapter, and the Bible passage referenced. Make note of any additional sections or issues that you'd like to incorporate into the discussion.
- As each session begins, try to get a sense of how many people have read the chapters for the week. Do not shame those who have not read, but it is helpful to know how much background information you need to supply for the discussion to go smoothly.
- If a few group members seem to dominate the discussion, particularly with their own personal stories, be intentional about redirecting the conversation and specifically encouraging quieter persons to speak. Do not push anyone to speak who is not comfortable, but sometimes people have trouble breaking into a discussion with more assertive voices.
- Allow a few moments for participants to reflect and respond to questions before offering your perspective or pointing them to a particular verse of Scripture or page of the book.

NOTES

Chapter 1: Contented People Know That External Circumstances Don't Determine Happiness

1. Sonja Lyubomirsky, *The How of Happiness: A New Approach to Getting the Life You Want* (New York: Penguin Books, 2008); Sonja Lyubomirsky, *The Myths of Happiness: What Should Make You Happy, but Doesn't, What Shouldn't Make You Happy, but Does* (New York: Penguin Books, 2014).
2. Martin Seligman, *Flourish: A Visionary New Understanding of Happiness and Well-Being* (New York: Atria Books, 2012), 226.
3. Lyubomirsky, *The How of Happiness*, 18.
4. Ibid., 17.
5. Ibid., 40.
6. Ibid., 43.
7. Ibid., 46.
8. Ibid., 41–42.
9. Ibid., 48.
10. Richard Layard, *Happiness: Lessons from a New Science* (New York: Penguin Books, 2006), 3.
11. Ibid., 29.
12. Ibid., 31.
13. Ibid., 36.
14. Ibid., 38.
15. Ibid., 62.

16. Martin Seligman, *Authentic Happiness: Using the New Positive Psychology to Realize Your Potential for Lasting Fulfillment* (New York: Atria Books, 2004), 49.

17. Ibid.

18. Ibid.

19. Ibid.

20. Ibid., 53.

21. Ibid., 58–59.

22. P. Brickman, D. Coates, and R. Janoff-Bulman, "Lottery Winners and Accident Victims: Is Happiness Relative?" *Journal of Personality and Social Psychology* 36 (1978): 917–27.

23. Seligman, *Authentic Happiness*, 58–59.

24. Ibid., 13.

25. Ibid., 49.

Chapter 2: Contented People Use Trials as Growth Opportunities

1. Sonja Lyubomirsky, *The How of Happiness: A New Approach to Getting the Life You Want* (New York: Penguin Books, 2008), 158–59.

Chapter 3: Contented People Cultivate Optimism

1. Martin Seligman, *Flourish: A Visionary New Understanding of Happiness and Well-Being* (New York: Atria Books, 2012), 33–34, 43.

2. Martin Seligman, *Authentic Happiness: Using the New Positive Psychology to Realize Your Potential for Lasting Fulfillment* (New York: Atria Books, 2004), 3–4.

3. Bob Dole, *One Soldier's Story* (New York: HarperCollins, 2005), 237.

4. Ibid., 244.

Chapter 4: Contented People Focus on the Present

1. Martin Seligman, *Authentic Happiness: Using the New Positive Psychology to Realize Your Potential for Lasting Fulfillment* (New York: Atria Books, 2004), 107.

2. Ibid., 102–21; Sonja Lyubomirsky, *The How of Happiness: A New Approach to Getting the Life You Want* (New York: Penguin Books, 2008), 180–204.

3. Robert Hastings, "The Station," accessed November 14, 2014, http://www.gettysburg.edu/dotAsset/7da4f91e–3473–4e09-b383 –0ad97a0b50d5.pdf.

4. Joe Kemp, "The Best Time of My Life," accessed November 14, 2014, http://www.great-inspirational-quotes.com/the-best-time-of -my-life.html.

Chapter 5: Contented People Practice Forgiveness

1. Martin Seligman, *Authentic Happiness: Using the New Positive Psychology to Realize Your Potential for Lasting Fulfillment* (New York: Atria Books, 2004), 76–77.

2. Mitch Albom, *The Five People You Meet in Heaven* (New York: Hyperion Books, 2003), 141.

3. Sonja Lyubomirsky, *The How of Happiness: A New Approach to Getting the Life You Want* (New York: Penguin Books, 2008), 172.

4. Anne Lamott, *Plan B: Further Thoughts on Faith* (New York: Riverhead Books, 2005), 45–55.

5. Lyubomirsky, *The How of Happiness*, 176.

6. Seligman, *Authentic Happiness*, 79–81.

7. Martin Thielen, *The Answer to Bad Religion Is Not No Religion: A Guide to Good Religion for Seekers, Skeptics, and Believers* (Louisville, KY: Westminster John Knox Press, 2014), 128–29.

Chapter 6: Contented People Practice Generosity

1. Sonja Lyubomirsky, *The How of Happiness: A New Approach to Getting the Life You Want* (New York: Penguin Books, 2008), 126.

2. Martin Seligman, *Flourish: A Visionary New Understanding of Happiness and Well-Being* (New York: Atria Books, 2012), 20.

3. Richard Layard, *Happiness: Lessons from a New Science* (New York: Penguin Books, 2006), 72.

4. John Huffman Jr., "The Generosity Factor," *Preaching: Leading the Church, Proclaiming the Word*, May/June 2007, accessed November 14, 2014, http://www.preaching.com/sermons/11547322.

Chapter 7: Contented People Nurture Relationships

1. Martin Seligman, *Flourish: A Visionary New Understanding of Happiness and Well-Being* (New York: Atria Books, 2012), 21.

2. Richard Layard, *Happiness: Lessons from a New Science* (New York: Penguin Books, 2006), 66.

3. Gretchen Rubin, *The Happiness Project: Or, Why I Spent a Year Trying to Sing in the Morning, Clean My Closets, Fight Right, Read Aristotle, and Generally Have More Fun* (New York: HarperCollins, 2009), 141.

4. Martin Seligman, *Authentic Happiness: Using the New Positive Psychology to Realize Your Potential for Lasting Fulfillment* (New York: Atria Books, 2004), 42.

5. Sonja Lyubomirsky, *The How of Happiness: A New Approach to Getting the Life You Want* (New York: Penguin Books, 2008), 125.

6. Will Miller, *Refrigerator Rights: Why We Need to Let People in Our Lives, Our Homes (and Our Refrigerators) . . . and How to Bring Even More Relationships into Our Lives* (Amherst, MA: White River Press, 2007).

7. Martin Thielen, *The Answer to Bad Religion Is Not No Religion: A Guide to Good Religion for Seekers, Skeptics, and Believers* (Louisville, KY: Westminster John Knox Press, 2014), 97.

Chapter 8: Contented People Express Gratitude

1. Martin Seligman, *Flourish: A Visionary New Understanding of Happiness and Well-Being* (New York: Atria Books, 2012), 30.

2. Sonja Lyubomirsky, *The How of Happiness: A New Approach to Getting the Life You Want* (New York: Penguin Books, 2008), 89.

3. Ibid., 15.

Chapter 9: Contented People Care for Their Bodies

1. Sonja Lyubomirsky, *The How of Happiness: A New Approach to Getting the Life You Want* (New York: Penguin Books, 2008), 244–45.

2. Ibid., 250.

3. Nancy Beach, *An Hour on Sunday: Creating Moments of Transformation and Wonder* (Grand Rapids, MI: Zondervan, 2004), 129.

Chapter 10: Contented People Care for Their Souls

1. Richard Layard, *Happiness: Lessons from a New Science* (New York: Penguin Books, 2006), 72.

2. Martin Seligman, *Authentic Happiness: Using the New Positive Psychology to Realize Your Potential for Lasting Fulfillment* (New York: Atria Books, 2004), 59.
3. Sonja Lyubomirsky, *The How of Happiness: A New Approach to Getting the Life You Want* (New York: Penguin Books, 2008), 228–39.
4. Barbara Brown Taylor, "Let There Be Night," *Time*, April 28, 2014, 40.
5. Fred Craddock, *The Cherry Log Sermons* (Louisville, KY: Westminster John Knox Press, 2001), 11–12.

ABOUT THE AUTHOR

Martin Thielen is author of the best-selling *What's the Least I Can Believe and Still Be a Christian? A Guide to What Matters Most*, rev. ed. (Louisville, KY: Westminster John Knox Press, 2012) and *The Answer to Bad Religion Is Not No Religion: A Guide to Good Religion for Seekers, Skeptics, and Believers* (Louisville, KY: Westminster John Knox Press, 2014). He also writes columns for MinistryMatters.com, Circuit Rider, and Net Results, among others. He is senior pastor of Cookeville United Methodist Church in Cookeville, Tennessee.

The author's website is www.GettingReadyForSunday .com. Here you will find preaching, worship, and pastoral leadership articles, sermons and sermon series, and other helpful information.

CPSIA information can be obtained at www.ICGtesting.com
Printed in the USA
LVOW11s0322140116

470544LV00004B/4/P

33029100930841

es *You* Happy?

"Martin Thielen's new book, *Searching for Happiness*, is a captivating read. I read it straight through in one sitting. Using Scripture, science, and personal experience, Thielen reminds us eloquently that happiness does not come from material things or external circumstances, but rather, real contentment comes from within us. At the end of the day, happiness is 'an inside job!'"

—JAMES W. MOORE, best-selling author and minister in residence at Highland Park United Methodist Church, Dallas, Texas

The key to happiness is being rich, successful, and beautiful. . . *right*? Best-selling author Martin Thielen insists that this is far from the truth.

Using psychological research, personal anecdotes, and Scripture, Thielen describes ten practices that *do* contribute to happiness in this easy-to-read book. Instead of aiming to make more money, Thielen contends that expressing gratitude and cultivating optimism are surer paths to joy. Rather than focusing on constant advancement in our careers, let's practice our ability to forgive, to be generous, and to use trials as growth opportunities. These lessons, and much more, help readers who may be dissatisfied in their lives see that authentic contentment is closer than they ever imagined.

The book features a guide for group or individual study, which includes questions for reflection and a challenge for each individual to reflect on during the week.

MARTIN THIELEN is author of the best-selling *What's the Least I Can Believe and Still Be a Christian?* and *The Answer to Bad Religion Is Not No Religion.* He frequently writes for MinistryMatters.com, *Circuit Rider*, and Net Results, among others. He is Senior Pastor of Cookeville United Methodist Church in Cookeville, Tennessee. He offers worship and preaching ideas at www.GettingReadyForSunday.com.

Self-Help / Christian Living
ISBN-13: 978-0-664-23712-7

9 780664 237127

www.wjkbooks.com

WJK